*To Uncle Micheal
Love From
Lily x*

BUSTA RHYME

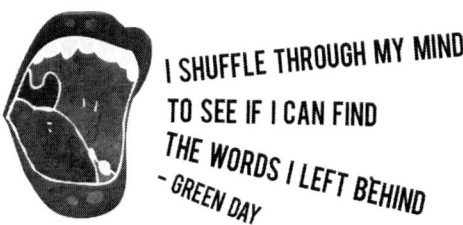

I SHUFFLE THROUGH MY MIND
TO SEE IF I CAN FIND
THE WORDS I LEFT BEHIND
- GREEN DAY

THE POET WITHIN

Edited By Lottie Boreham

First published in Great Britain in 2017 by:

Coltsfoot Drive
Peterborough
PE2 9BF
Telephone: 01733 890066
Website: www.youngwriters.co.uk

All Rights Reserved
Book Design by Ashley Janson
© Copyright Contributors 2017
SB ISBN 978-1-78624-915-9
Printed and bound in the UK by BookPrintingUK
Website: www.bookprintinguk.com
YB0304N

FOREWORD

Welcome Reader,

For Young Writers' latest competition, *Busta Rhyme*, we challenged secondary school pupils to take inspiration from the world around them, whether from the news, their own lives or even songs, and write a poem on any subject of their choice. They rose to the challenge magnificently, with young writers up and down the country displaying their poetic flair.

We chose poems for publication based on style, expression, imagination and technical skill. The result is this entertaining collection full of diverse and imaginative poetry which covers a variety of topics - from favourite things and seasons to more serious subjects such as bullying and war. Using poetry as their tool, the young writers have taken this opportunity to express their thoughts and feelings through verse. This anthology is also a delightful keepsake to look back on in years to come.

Here at Young Writers our aim is to encourage creativity in the next generation and to inspire a love of the written word, so it's great to get such an amazing response, with some absolutely fantastic poems. I'd like to congratulate all the young poets in this anthology, I hope this inspires them to continue with their creative writing.

Lottie Boreham

CONTENTS

Independent Entries

Deborah Fateye (13)	1
Michaela Wyatt (12)	2
Alex Moyer (15)	4
Alice Annie Elizabeth Jackson (12)	5

Abbey Christian Brothers Grammar School, Newry

Kyle James Byrne (13)	6
Fionntán Gregory (13)	8

Ballyclare Secondary School, Ballyclare

Catherine Hill (14)	9

Forest House School, Leicester

Henry Sharman-Lowe (16)	11

Gosford Hill School, Kidlington

Lauren Eames (16)	12

Highlands School, London

Richmond Mawutor (14)	13
Oliwia Bugno (14)	14
Nicholas Papanicolaou	20
Ellie Davies	23
Zara Iqbal	24
Ocean Bolasingh (13)	26
Marianna Martin (14)	28
Lily Shaw (14)	31

Liana Chowdhury (13)	32
Carla Sophia Charalambous	34
Imogen Elizabeth Russell (13)	36
Isabel Davies	38
Tilly Balenger	40
Madi Tait (13)	42
Caterina Thompson (13)	44
Thomas Halstead	46
Michela Louise Foramacchi (13)	47
Armantas Mankevicius (14)	48
Lois Kozinos	50
David Joseph Britton (13)	51
Nicholas Tofallis	52
Olivia Sharpe (14)	54
Juliet Taaffe	55
Thea Haines	56
Ayse Orhan-Pennell (13)	58
George Athanasiou (13)	60
Owen Edwards	61
Holly Tyrrell (14)	62
Raqiya Cali	63
Hannah Porter (14)	64
Jack Dewhirst (13)	65
Shobhana Singarayer	66
Zara Satti	67
Ashni Backory	68
Evan Eldridge	69
Charlotte Dodd	70
Hala Abughazza	71
Grace Kent	72
Moneera Ali (14)	73
Marley-Marie Stewart (13)	74
Frankie Merrick (14)	75
Caitlin Flanagan	76
Dogus Grosu (13)	77

Megan Bicknell (13)	78
Baysu Kurt (14)	79
Khushi Khatry	80
Sifa Sahiner (13)	81
Owen Sinclair Jones (13)	82
Mia Arney (13)	83
Rianna Biswas (14)	84
Olivia Koublis-Hakki	85
Naomi Leighton (13)	86
Emre Dixon (13)	87
Chinwe Opurum-Kpandi (13)	88
Nathaniel Angate (14)	89
Ryan McCowen	90
Katy Grande	91
Miles Holder	92
Alex Gendler Smith (14)	93
Mackenzie Joy (13)	94
Andre Charles	95
David Kourides	96
Henry Wackett (13)	97
Clare Hamid (13)	98
Antony Patrick Milligan (13)	99
Kamoliddin Usman (13)	100
Eleni Petinou (14)	101

Islay High School, Isle Of Islay

Nicholas Weatherhogg (13)	102
Sarah Eve MacPherson (12)	104
Anwen Baker (13)	105
Emily Mackie (13)	106
Amy Want (13)	107
Joseph Hamilton (11)	108

Jamea Al Kauthar, Lancaster

Asmaa Mohamed (13)	109
Kareena Yasmin (13)	110
Tayyibah Ahmed (13)	112
Halima Shazad Sadia (13)	113
Aamna Nadeem Chouhdry (14)	114
Yumna Razick (13)	115
Sumayya Ali (13)	116
Ferdousi Yasmin (13)	117

Fathima Mohamed Rila (13)	118
Amina Begum (13)	119
Aamna Rehman (13)	120
Mahima Begum (13)	121

Merchiston Castle School, Edinburgh

Niles Kinder (13)	122
Johnnie Dodds (13)	123
Toby Gray (13)	124
Archie MacLean-Bristol (13)	125
James Gilding (12)	126
Adam Leighton (14)	128
Tom Channing (14)	129
Neil MacPherson (13)	130
Ocean Nash (11)	131
Tom Logan (13)	132

Oaklands Catholic School & Sixth Form College, Waterlooville

Ruthie Quinn (11)	133

St Benedict's Catholic College, Colchester

Grace Lewis (12)	134
Rijin Thomas Rajan (11)	137
Natasha Gail Escabarte (13)	138
Gareth Moriarty	140
Orla Gosling-Campbell (12)	142
Luc Hémeury (12)	145
Benita Mehri (12)	146
Anjelina Bown (13)	148
Genevieve Wersong (14)	150
Inge-Maria C Botha (13)	152
Mia Andrea Patterson (14)	154
James Stirling (12)	156
Olivia Farry (13)	158
Tristan Louis Perera (13)	160
Tom Brown (14)	162
Harry Owen Thomas (12)	163
Ama Wellahewage (13)	164

Bandi Cserep (13)	165
Lucy Lester (12)	166
Julian Olivagi (13)	167
Amisha Muhandiramge (12)	168
Maddie Barrell (13)	169
Louis Gannon	170
Meadow Giles (13)	171
Matthew Hull (12)	172
Lyle Gabriel Miano (12)	173
Thomas Cresswell (11)	174
Luke Campbell (13)	175
Amaia Lilia Jane D'Souza (13)	176
Daniella Obianuju Akpiama (13)	178
Niamh Mary O'Neill (14)	179
Mya Obwoya (12)	180
Abigail Rose Wetton (12)	181
Shania Hughes (12)	182
Ore Ayanbadejo (12)	183
George Sibthorp (13)	184
Freya Richardson (13)	185
Nicole Lentas (13)	186
Mary Richardson (11)	187
Francesca Jacks (13)	188
James Christopher Beattie (12)	189
Shalom Awesu (13)	190
Chardonnay Fuller (12)	191
Tilly Leach (11)	192
Manny Roarty (12)	193
Lalea Garcia Radones (12)	194
Victoria Kessel (11)	195
Chloe Claxton (11)	196
Anna Kelpi (13)	197
Shanice Acheamponmah (11)	198
Jonpaul Fisher (13)	199

St Ronan's College, Lurgan

Eva Callaghan (14)	200
Aoife Elliott (17)	202
Clíodhna McDonald (14)	203
Sian Heaney (14)	204
Mikey McCann (14)	205
Aine Callaghan (16)	206
Andrew Cooper (14)	207
Daire Kieran Campbell (14)	208
Lauren Wilson	209

THE POEMS

Spreading Kindness

A homeless man scrunches on the filthy ground staring at the sky,
His face masked with dirt,
His hair, thick locks that hang loosely on his head,
It's unknown what tomorrow may bring;
But he still does well,

His helping hand intrigues the nation,
'What has he to be happy about?' they sneer,
He has no money,
Their judgmental faces close around him,
Watching his every move,
But he refuses to care,
He has nothing to give but still helps the nation,

However there's a fat man sitting by the crackling flame,
His hand on his belly, laughing and his other on piles of money,
Spent on only the best food and a pointless mansion,
One day he passes by the homeless man and flinches,
His hand tight on his money,
The homeless man raises his hand,
Showing the sign *In Need? Please Help Yourself*,
He pointed to pennies that lay beside him
No one has ever become poor by giving,
Have they?

Deborah Fateye (13)

Save Our World

Look, look at our world now
This planet which belongs to you and I somehow
Believed that God made this beautiful place
Where peace, prosperity, pity should be comprehended in this case
But peace is an immense question to us
It is an issue that must be accomplished by thus
In history, such a mystery
A topic which is very blistery, and can be sophistry
We have never found agreement
But we tried fighting for it with the government
We achieved to endure through World War One and Two
But will the death and distress of today lead to World War Three for me and you?
As you know, poppies are used to show our dedication
But these poppies' red petals are the soldier's profound, dark, enflamed blood of deprivation
The tears that are spread today are like sinuous waterfalls of mourn
Just because of the number of deaths occurring so fast like babies being born
But what are we as individuals doing to assist?
Just watching our loved ones perishing - that's not right we must insist
The best preparation for tomorrow is doing your best today
A quote from Jackson Brown that you should follow every day

So try and turn this world into a better place
Save our world and let no more blood be shed, show grace.

Michaela Wyatt (12)

Charity Shop Books

There is nothing more that I adore
Than a book that comes from a charity shop
It is not clear what for
With their yellowed pages and the cracked spines
As how could these features be adored?

Well maybe it's something that can't be seen
The book's hidden history
Where has it come from?
Where has it been?
Who was the owner?
Why is it here?

You can tell with some who the owners were
Students marking numbers next to the Roman Numerals
Pencils underlining useful quotes
For an essay?
For an exam?
I will never know

Some you can tell were just no longer used;
Little brick-like things
This edition first published in 1982

For all these reasons I adore
Old charity shop books and I know
That the one pound, eighty-two pence I pay
Helps other people in a special way.

Alex Moyer (15)

Society

How can I say I'm pretty when I have no likes?
How can I say I'm funny when I've got no loops on vine?
How can I say I'm clever when all my grades are Bs?
How can happiness be said to be a disease?
For everyone else has it in abundance
Yet I am free,
Because I do not fall into society,
Yet I have to live on
Being 'funny and free'
Because I'm not part of society,
My friends aren't free.

Alice Annie Elizabeth Jackson (12)

Our Earth Is Crumbling Apart

As the sun rises for a new dawn, a new day
Its power is immensely increasing due to the acts;
The acts us humans partake in from day to day
Destroying our environment; enclosing it in dismay

As the polar bear prowls for a fantastic feast
It is oblivious to the danger it faces
From the hunters to the sun's increasing power, these dangers are decreasing the survivors
The survivors that are overlooked by the civilians under the sun

Unaware of the circumstances ahead, the Amazon tree frog jumps across the leaves
Of the mighty, colossal forest that surrounds, as a spider surrounded by a flock of birds
Oblivious to the circumstances that lay ahead; the creature spies out for his next feast
Although the hunters come from behind and snatch him from his habitat
As a child picking a sweet from a candy store would
The colossal forest now as empty as a dark, dingy mansion on a ghostly hill

As the flock of geese soar through the gas infused sky
Abandoned by the other specials of birds; as they soar through the sky
Deserted as they inhale the toxic gases; which smother the birds to death

The geese drop out of the atmosphere; as harsh as stones falling into water
As the civilian outlooks the event unfolding, his face forms a cheeky grin which conceals an evil laugh
The atmosphere is engulfed with gas and is oblivious to the fumes it will be engulfed by next

Why do we do this to our own planet?
It contains living creatures that share the Earth with us
The clumsy hunter looking for a fortune
The evil grin on the entrepreneur's face as he
makes a fortune
Whilst releasing harmful fumes into the atmosphere
It is time to take responsibility for these actions that are crumbling our planet apart
After all, we are the biggest murderer on our planet
as time evolved
We have to remember that we are one species sharing the planet with others
It is time to take action!

Kyle James Byrne (13)
Abbey Christian Brothers Grammar School, Newry

We Matter Too

Wouldn't you think that it's absurd
That sometimes kids can't contribute a word
That people shaping a better tomorrow
Get shot down by adults, causing us sorrow

Whether big or small, we're all the same
From those unknown or those adorned by fame
Children can pray, children have views
We can relay information, pass on news

If I were to tell you, 'Children could change the world.'
Would you scorn in disgust, or give us a word?
We can comprehend, we have opinions too
We don't just ensconce and attend cartoons

We have emotions, each of us have feelings
Children have perspectives, views, ways of healing
Healing broken devotions, torn apart by war
Because children have opinions, we all have a core

We are all akin, whether from here or there
We are in need of freedom, in need of being heard
We can speak free, we can speak true
I recognise this, as we matter too.

Fionntán Gregory (13)
Abbey Christian Brothers Grammar School, Newry

The Weapon

You see, I have a bump on my fourth finger
The friction from my pen caused the mountain to arise from my skin
I write the essays, equations, stories and calculations
And my little bump stands
A proud soldier
It is proof of that one day I could do something great

You see, there is a little girl in Ethiopia who has a bump on her baby toe
The friction from the rough rocky ground caused it to arise from her skin
She walks six kilometres a day to quench her family's thirst
Her bump grows
On tender, petite feet
It is proof of the barrier that separates her from
life's essentials

When the buzzing of your alarm blares through your ears
Dawn's light creeping through your safe house
Don't groan
Don't moan
Take your pen and pencil and write for the children who can't
Read for the ones who don't know how to
Because with this, you have the ultimate weapon

One day
We will be the reason every child has a little bump on their finger
We are the doctors, the writers, the politicians, the teachers
We will tackle the problems we face now, head first.

Catherine Hill (14)
Ballyclare Secondary School, Ballyclare

A Call Of Vacuous Minds

Fail not, to the call of a whistle
To clamber up and over, to be engulfed into smoke
Those who would emerge, became that of bloodied ghosts
A city of children who do not smile
A city of children who do not quiver and fall to the crushing of their own knees
Fail not, to the call of a whistle
The looming dark, a vulture, a testament to the place which emits no joys and ambition
But as heinous acts seep from the cavity that binds us
Fail not, to the call of a whistle
But give some thought, to being the one who bears the whistle itself.

Henry Sharman-Lowe (16)
Forest House School, Leicester

Qu'est-Ce Que J'ai Fait?

In a circle we sit
My fellow students and I
A glare centred on the back of my head
I can hardly speak
Nor make a sound
As the teacher stares me into the ground

So I got it wrong
What's the fuss?
I just said salut instead of ca va
But now a vein's popping out of her head
Seriously, is this all because of what I said?

Blondie's snickering
Down at the front
Though quickly silenced
When she bears the brunt
Of that icy glare
So cold, so slick
I think I'd better get out of this quick

'Sorry miss,' is my quick reply
'I swear I'll try harder next time!'
'See that you do,' is her snide reply
'Or I assure you, you'll never see a break time!'

Lauren Eames (16)
Gosford Hill School, Kidlington

Our Evil

We are a race of hate, greed, evil and destruction
We turn a blind eye to those who deteriorate in the
mists of famine
Our television are masks of the real world that surrounds us
A world where children sleep with imagery of death
in their minds

We gaze on as a great nation crumbles in the wake of their
own ignorance
I see my brothers gunning down each other because they
wear different uniform
They sleep in fear never knowing if the bombs will finally
lock on them
Then the ear-piercing screams of parents burying
their children

We forget about those who shrivel with empty stomachs
Mothers who are struggling to feed their young because the
land fails them
Children who shriek in terror as the sounds of dive bombers
fill the sky
Then our brother and sisters fall as the ground beneath
them explodes

We shield our eyes from those who harm one another with
sharp metal objects
People who don't see the dark side of their action
One day we will regret our barbaric ways
Or dwell in the eternal bliss of hellfire.

Richmond Mawutor (14)
Highlands School, London

Lost Souls

That girl?
Who claims love isn't real
And that she doesn't need it?
She needs it more than anyone
She fears not being wanted
And doesn't want to be on the receiving end
Of the pain accompanying it
So she broke her own heart
Before anyone else could
That girl is me

My emotions were enslaved to her
She had my whole being captured
It was tragically beautiful
The fact that I could never be with
The one person who gave me purpose
I wanted to give back the happiness
To the one person who showed me what it was
Her
I couldn't physically breathe at the sight of her
She made me cry
Scream, shout
And fall in love with her
Without even knowing

My chest is getting tighter
And my breaths are getting heavier
Something as easy as breathing
Is a hard task to accomplish right now
Let alone trying to control
The tear ducts in your eyes
And trusting yourself
To not let them spill
I don't understand
Or even know why I feel like this
Like you're just nothing
And no one could give a damn about you
Even though you know that's not the case
Regarding some, if not all people
And you're just thinking irrational thoughts

Missing her came in pills
And by this point
I was drugged
I was at my ultimate high
Wishing I was injecting her love for me in my veins
Instead of this poison
These toxins entered my system
And could do nothing
But let them control my body
Not that that's the first time that I let something
Or rather someone
Control my own body

My thoughts
My emotions

If I would have known any better
I would have said bye
On the same day I said hi
But I didn't know any better
And I still don't
Because I'm still here
On my knees
Begging that she won't pull the trigger
Even though I gave her the gun

I think the reason as to why I'm so scared of losing her
Is that I know I don't want another person
To imprint their kiss
On my lips
I don't want their hands
To take the place of hers
I don't want them to erase her touch
From my skin
I want her touch to remain
Like a beautiful, dark tattoo on my body
With hidden secrets
And a story behind it
So her touch will permanently stay on me
For as long as I live
With no fear of anyone replacing it

But instead
Her touch stayed on me
Like a disgusting scar
Fearful of anyone touching it
I tried to wash it away
To cover her mark
I don't let anyone get too close
Because I'm scared
I never asked for that

She could taste the sadness in my kiss
She could hear it in my laugh
When my tears fell
That's when she lost it
That's when I lost it
Her arms were my home that day
She kept me warm
But I still couldn't feel
I became immune to it
'It' being everything
Everything apart from pain
Every inch of me was under pain's commands
All I knew was the never-ending shouts
And constant tears
If only I knew how much her heart was breaking
With every melancholic sound my lips let out
She wanted to make my sadness go away
As easy as it came

She was the mitochondria of my being
The electricity in my veins
The pain in my tears
The story of my mind
She was the voice of my laugh
She was the words written across my battered journal
The sentences still having yet to fathom an order
She was my 3am heartbreak
And 2pm rendezvous

It's black and white for me
I'm either too clingy
Or too distant
I either speak too much
Or bite my tongue
And let silence take the place of me
I either eat too much
Or not at all
I've never known what grey is
But one thing for sure
It's always her on my mind

She was a beauty
Her eyes were green
Her heart was one of gold
Anyone would be lucky to captivate it
And I was the lucky one

I didn't want to admit to myself
That I was getting better
I didn't want to admit
That she was the reason why
I wasn't ready to face the fact that -
If she left me
I'd turn into a sad nothing
Because when she's with me
I'm a happy something
My soul literally needs her to stay
She's my breath of fresh air
In this polluted world
I often forgot how to breathe
And it was always because of her.

Oliwia Bugno (14)
Highlands School, London

Freedom In Madness

The dying wife screams at night
While the baby gasps for breaths
I stand in fright and try to fight
I must confront their deaths

I have to pay debts so high
And cannot afford to stay
I stand and fight but must not cry
And so can only pray

Each day begins work and labour
And I face them with dismay
My life lacks any flavour
But a bitter taste of grey

Until one day it gets so bad
I lose all hope to give
But one sweet taste of freedom makes me think
Have I really lived?

I feel the kindling of ecstasy
Flare inside of me
It consumes me so stresslessly
And I finally feel free

And now the warm fire burns bright
I finally see a path
A path leading to pure light
Now I start to laugh

At first only a chuckle
But then a mighty roar
I finally feel free of struggle
Rid of endless war

My life was bland
But I now walk, hand in hand
With my madness
For evermore

My hysteric grin
Like a harlequin's
Will forever be worn
In pride across my face

I have no age
Feel no pain
My madness has engulfed me
I ascend to sweet insanity

And now I've succumbed
But why ever run?
I'm able to choose my own path

Perhaps it was always a part of me
Buried very deep inside
But now I've been freed
And I can put the past behind

If I'm to have a past again
I'd prefer it to be multiple choice
You see, that's the thing, about being sane
There's never room to rejoice

I hear the stories about democracy
Society, where everyone has a choice
But, you see, that's hypocrisy
Because no matter how loud you are
They can barely hear your voice

So I prefer chaos
Because chaos is fair
And you can do as you wish
Without the trouble of care

Why imprison yourself behind a mask
When we're all mad inside
Why bottle your freedom in a flask
When you could cast your restraints aside?

Nicholas Papanicolaou
Highlands School, London

Poem In The Past

In the past we thought no one is dying any more for what they believe in
In the past we said no more women are being discriminated against for who they are
In the past we believed, because that's what they told us
In the past, or is it just the beginning of all this fuss?
Is it the truth that we have all been lying to ourselves?
Is it true that we have all fallen slaves to
what the news says?
Are there still people getting shot for what they believe in?
Are there still people being told what they are is a sin?
Are there still children working like slaves in the factories?
Is there still no one believing that this is a tragedy?
Is it true that our story books have been lying?
Are there still so many people unreservedly dying?
Are these the questions that still haunt our day?
Or is this a way of making us pay?
Is there a way to change this around?
Or are we stuck hopelessly on the ground?
Is there anything we can do or are we stuck in this tragedy?
Can we reverse or are we left in this
black and white catastrophe?

Ellie Davies
Highlands School, London

Her Name Was Essence...

Lying was her language.
It ran right through her blood.
Her lies tread deep within the soul.
They would scar your heart for life.

It wasn't her, it was them.
They converted her.
It was like there was a tiny wisp of her left inside,
Screaming to get out.

She made you bring down your defences;
Then you were exposed vulnerability.
She took you apart from the inside out.
You were the puppet and she was the master.

She played all kinds of twisted games.
The games they taught her how to play.
And when you tried to play their game,
Defeat hit you like a crashing wave.

You think you could have played their games?
Well, you couldn't have thought more wrong.
There is no worse game to play,
Than the maze of manipulation

But there came the time I took the chance.
I grasped it with both hands.
But the fire of her psychopathic ways,
Burned me down to cinders.

She spun and spun a new web of lies.
But they all came ploughing down,
Because I arose from the ashes,
Ready to face the devil.

Her pursuers turned and fled,
The only ones she'd abide.
She was left with intense neglect,
Her carcass filled with sorrow.

I remember that day so clearly,
She was all alone at lunch.
It began to pour with rain,
Like she was weeping about what she had done.

Most would say she deserved it,
But I saw the greater good.
I stood by her and all her worries,
I became her one and only friend.

Now twenty years later here we are.
Only I saw what was truly inside,
Essence was filled with empathy and love.
I had reconstructed her and her tales.

She supported me as I have her,
We are together as one,
Essence and faith,
The weaver of lies and the amnesty angel.

Zara Iqbal
Highlands School, London

Run, Ocean, Run

'Run, Ocean, run!' Funny phrase that
I hear it too often, it's that one phrase that's all I need for motivation
To help push me into further motion.

It's that klaxon that really sinks in;
The thing loud enough to place me in a spin
But the words are more effective than anything at all
And each one grows more effective
More and more and more...

'On your marks!': Is the one that really sinks in your head
Just so you know that you're the best!
'Set,' is the one that really keeps you ready
Just so you know that you can always be steady
Then here comes, 'Go!'
My favourite word, the word that really makes you run
'Run, run, run, as fast as you can.'
Yeah run and never look back
In a race, you think you may win
But you can so easily lose
But just try your best and you make it through,
and you will not ever feel so blue.
So I run and run to make my fame tall,
just to tumble and not to fall.

'Don't give up, don't give up!' said my coach,
just so he knows I will not lose hope
So I run and I run like I've never run before;
running like a cheetah chasing after boar
And as I run these words I recite, 'Run, Ocean, run!'

As I run I look aside,
seeing all the other speedsters running just behind,
so I pick up my pace just one pace more,
really running towards the end, more and more and more.
So I reach the end and all I see,
is one proud coach smiling at me.
And I feel the wind finally jump off my face,
staring at my medal, as proud as my coach was of me,
and as I stare I recite, 'Run, Ocean, run!'

Ocean Bolasingh (13)
Highlands School, London

Suicide Sky

The sky was so blue
But it wasn't blue any longer
The sky ascended our atmosphere
And forged a new shade of blue

Every time that sky
Comes back into my mind
The colours switch
The blue gets bluer
And the horizon widens

The ink spot in that new blue sky
Was my kite
As it rose higher
And entered our skyline

The last time I flew a kite
The time when blue wasn't the ocean
It wasn't a mood
It wasn't a rainy day
And it wasn't the sky
And the sky was just the sky

I looked up as my mind flew away
But my feet were hard on the ground
My kite was flying as high
As the rope would let it go

I was walking on a world
No longer on my own

The last time I flew a kite
I wasn't flying a kite

The last time I flew a kite
The sky wasn't blue
And the sky wasn't inside me
Maybe I made it up
Maybe it was cloudy

As my kite rose higher
I know I saw that blue
And at that moment
Colour splashed into my black and white life
Standing in the middle of nowhere
With the wind in my face
I lost myself

That blue wasn't the ocean
A mood
A rainy day
Or the sky
But it had nothing to do with you
Or your death
It only had to do with me
Which is why I realised

As my kite rose higher
Into that impossible blue
I wondered how we never flew
Kites together.

Marianna Martin (14)
Highlands School, London

Dreams

Every move we make and every breath we take
We're always being watched; judged and criticised
We always feel as if we have someone to impress
Someone to lead or someone to satisfy
We feel like we have to make every moment a happy one
Make every moment count

We're brainwashed into thinking we have to live up to such high standards
And if we don't reach these standards we are just
not good enough
Brainwashed into thinking that everyone is equal
That everyone is the same and everyone deserves
a second chance
Our dreams are crushed by the reality of society
The reality of our status

Our friends may seem like they're real and loyal
But we always find ourselves pulling the knives they stabbed out of our backs
We always find the people that know the least about us
Always have the most to say
And we always find ourselves forgiving the same people
Having the same problems, being snapped back into reality over and over
And never reaching our dreams.

Lily Shaw (14)
Highlands School, London

Imaginary Friends

I sit at home, all alone
No one to talk to
Nowhere to go
I wait for him, as time goes by, *tick, tock, tick, tock*

I wait for him but there is still no sign
I turn around, finding something to do
Then he appears out the blue
Hair as dark as chocolate, skin as sweet as honey
And eyes twinkling like stars in the night sky

My face starts to light up the dark
I walk toward him floating on cloud nine
Knowing that this knight in shining armour was mine

We walk and talk
Along the river bank of where we first met
Holding hands side by side
Laughing uncontrollably without a sweat

As the sun climbs down the hill, we stroll back to my house
Still holding hands side by side
He looks into my eyes, about to say goodbye
But my mum's voice calls out
Breaking me out of my fantasy

'What are you staring at?' she asks, questioning me
'My best friend,' I say, pointing at him
'But there's no one there,' she replies confusingly

I turn back to where I last saw him
Gone, vanished, disappeared into thin air
I call out his name, once, twice
Desperate to find him but he's nowhere to be seen
I sink to the floor
Tears running down my face
For I knew that was the last time that I could spend
With my one and only imaginary friend.

Liana Chowdhury (13)
Highlands School, London

Lose The Mask

Do you need to wear a mask?
Do you need to hide the imperfections of your complexion?
I mean, it doesn't change your whole personality, or better your mentality.

We are not on the production line to look the same,
or to be identical,
or to act and be perfect in every way.

You see, we are not supposed to be perfect,
or made up of metaphors.
Instead, we are made up of flesh, blood and bone with eyes that are meant to see.
Eyes that are blind, blind to who we actually are.
We are blind to the truth.

Do you need a powder to make your face more glowing?
Or two heated fingers to make your hair more flowing?
Is this because we don't want to look incorrect, or because we don't want to feel neglect?

Blind and brainwashed of how we should look and
not who we are.
But what you want to be and what you want to do.

Do you remember the fairytale that your mum told you, of a princess and the prince charming?
Of how she was perfect and how she got what she wanted?

You see, we're not like that.
We're not going to be perfect and find love straight away.

Instead we paint our eyes to hide behind, or try to perfect our blemishes.
We are not drawings that can be erased, but human beings that are all unique in our own, different way...

Carla Sophia Charalambous
Highlands School, London

Untitled

One night in August
I met a girl
Under clear skies
At the end of the world

She was a question mark
She was strange
She was all I had
So I loved her

She drank cheap gin
While I sipped water
I was my parent's son
But she was no one's daughter

She was a liar
She was a mess
She was like modern art
And I loved her

One night in April
I had some news
Which shattered my idyll
And put me in her shoes

I had stopped shaking
And cried all my tears
I was numb
And I loved her

I called her over
'I'm ready,' I lied
She sat down beside me
And looked in my eyes

She pulled something shiny out of her bag
My eyes were fixed on what she held in her hand
She said, 'These needles are popping lives like balloons
This is poison I'm putting in you.'

She was dangerous
This wasn't a game
People died of this
And I loved her

And yes, black happiness killed me
And she has to live with that pain
But she was the best of modern art
And I will always, always love her.

Imogen Elizabeth Russell (13)
Highlands School, London

The Mirror

In front of the mirror
did a young girl stand,
thinking and wanting to understand,
why society wanted her to be
all the things that she could never see.

The hated reflection was all she could notice
dark, loathing thoughts swarmed like locusts.
in front of the mirror she started to cry
wishing her imperfections would shrivel and die.

She thought to herself, why not change,
why not just rearrange
the parts of herself she could not stand
and recreate her image to look splendidly grand?

When she was done the reflection she saw
was no longer a person like her any more
but someone confident, dominant
pretty and strong,
but then she realised that what she saw was wrong.

Finally, she thought of society's tom foolery
and that she was gorgeous without make-up or jewellery.
She knew that one day that in her own skin
she would unlock the magic hidden within.

In front of the mirror stood a new girl
with all of her flaws she watched beauty unfurl,
the reflection before her although irrefutable
she knew deep down she was in fact
beautiful.

Isabel Davies
Highlands School, London

Inside Their Heads

To really tell this story
We must start at the end
I'm sad to say this story
Must begin with an empty bed

Footsteps on the pavement
One, two, three
He's filled his head with dreams
To hide his anxiety

The rope is tied
All she wanted was a smile
Scarred wrists and bleeding thighs
Silver blades and suicide

Is she awake?
Is she asleep?
No matter, she still hears the screams
The punishment for stupid wars
PTSD

Has he washed his hands enough?
Should he wash once more?
Though he cleans the germs off
This OCD is rotten to the core

One day near death, the next he's up
These deadly highs and lows

Bipolar uses him as a weapon
To control both friends and foe

These disorders don't define them
Much like the colour of their skin
Their stories are yet to be told
The endings could be paved in gold

To really tell his story
We must end at the beginning
I am happy to say this story
Ends with joyful tears and singing.

Tilly Balenger
Highlands School, London

Change

Not many thirteen-year-olds know what they want to be
When they grow up, they see
I do, at least I thought I did

Yesterday after hours of holding the correct posture
So I didn't have a big bum, a fat stomach or wide legs

I was told to give up
Enough was enough
For the person I had trusted the most had just given up

Legs too wide, bum too big, stomach too fat
I'll never be able to do a grand jete
Or execute a half decent arabesque

Looking like me
But I won't let this be

So I'll change
However change can range
Small change, big change or sometimes
Damaging change

Change or I won't succeed
Change or I'll be filled with greed
So I changed, but soon after I really found out
How much change can range

Rib bones on show
Neck bones all a bow
Legs all slim
And feet all bruised in

I guess change can be good
But if I ever want to soar
Becoming anorexic
Will only leave me near dead on the floor.

Madi Tait (13)
Highlands School, London

Borders

It's closed
Everywhere we seem to go
It's closed
We travel hours on end but eventually
It's closed

I guess nobody wants us
It's not like we can just take a train or a bus
We're stuck in the middle of the desert, the sea
We're stuck, never able to be

We're filled with hopes and dreams
But it just always seems
That they're meant to be destroyed; it's closed
And so, the wind blows
Our boat goes to the next border to be closed

My mum says we will find a place someday
I start to think, *How cliché*

We can find a place that's small and just right
If that ever happens it will sure be a sight
It happens so much that now I just suppose
Every single boarder will be closed

What's wrong with us?
Our skin, colour, race?
Why do we always have to be on the chase?

We will never get it, *Our dream home*
As I always say
It will be closed.

Caterina Thompson (13)
Highlands School, London

Donald Trump

So it's come to this I guess
To choose the lesser of two evils?
Politics has become a joke no less
When our vote creates the stress

If Clinton wins, of which I doubt
She's got too many dirty stories
She does know a lot about American politics
But she doesn't have the money to rally the protests

The hype about Trump
Has us down in the dumps
There's not much we can do to stop him
All we can do is grump and frump

As for the black people
Well we know they hate his guts
The burning of their trust
Soon he'll claim that he forgot

And as for good old Mexico
The country full of 'drug dealers and rapists'
Who knows how big the wall will be
But how will he get his South American liberty?

So it comes to choosing a president
America has to make a wise decision
Who will we choose, whose attempt
A businessman or another office seeker?

Thomas Halstead
Highlands School, London

First World Problems

'It's too hot outside, but too cold in the classroom.'
'It's too cold outside, but we don't have any heating!'
'My mum bought me new shoes, but she bought the wrong ones!'
'I wanted new shoes but my mum said she couldn't afford them.'
'I had to get the bus all the way to school!'
'I have to walk two miles to get water.'
'There's nothing on TV.'
'I don't know what that is.'
'My phone's about to die.'
'And so are many kids.'
'My purse is so heavy with all this spare change.'
'I never know if I'll see tomorrow - I'd sure like a change.'

As the night sings its lullaby
To you in your sleep
Somewhere in the world
A starving child curls and weeps
So wake up from your slumber
And put yourself in their shoes
Hoping to improve their lives
Not to be the headline of BBC news...

Michela Louise Foramacchi (13)
Highlands School, London

My Poem

Mr Trump, a candidate to become president
Donald Trump is his name.
His rival, the better in the world's opinions, Ms Clinton
Hillary Clinton is her name.

Donald Trump has abused humans
Women to be precise.
His rival has a past
A dark one in disguise.

The man, the strong one,
Accusing her of the bad,
But she stayed positive
While defending from the misleader.

Donald Trump rejecting his abuse,
Looking into making himself better use.
His political insanity becomes immense and huge,
And the crowds shout out all the boos.

His upsetting words,
Impact the people,
Causing more anger,
Leading to pain inside.

He says he helps the women,
Inside he knows he doesn't.
Trump accuses every one of the wrong,
To protect his own wrong.

He makes up lies,
Makes himself look nice,
He tries and tries,
And is not able to rise.

Armantas Mankevicius (14)
Highlands School, London

Does Girl Mean Weak?

I am the same yet different
I hear what people say
I am abused for who and what I am
Is that really okay?

I have been looking for jobs
Searching 'help wanted' posters down every street
Yet I am verbally attacked by what they say,
'Oh, you won't do, a big, strong man is what we need.'

Why can't males be the princess and girls the
shining knight?
We are told from young we can be different
Yet we are told it's not right

We are divided in society, in a world where girl means weak
and boy an excuse
Where 'feminist' strikes up disgust
But 'meninist' strikes up a laugh

There's a dictionary of words females are named
Yet there are no male equivalents - isn't that strange?

A spinster is a less rude word, an old cat lady
But if males grow old without a spouse
He is a bachelor, not deemed crazy?

Lois Kozinos
Highlands School, London

You Need Hope And Justice

Look at the sea
I will tell you what you need
You need hope and justice
Because they are banging you to the ground
But can you hear that sound?
It's the sound of justice and hope
'Cause they are banging you to the ground
But can you hear that sound?
It's the sound of justice and hope
Three-sixty, no scope! You'll be catching them
In prison and they won't come round
But can you hear that sound?
The sound of justice

Look at the sea
Because all you see
Is fights and murders
Because all you have to do is stand up
And they won't be troubling you no more
Because all you gonna do is tell the world
What you need to do
Because all you want is plain justice
'Cause one day they'll be caught and I'll see justice, bro
Because if you believe in justice you can achieve justice.

David Joseph Britton (13)
Highlands School, London

Untitled

A hand is a hand
Which is violent and bland
A gun is a gun
Which is violent and not fun
You use your hand to pull the trigger

Violence might not change
Our hand sizes range
And who won't make this change
This month we may know

He is oh so arrogant
Racist, sexist and abusive
He wants his way and to kill in a click
His followers are thick

He doesn't know what he's in for
Biting into the earth's core
He thinks he is the man
I don't give a damn
Others think he's cool
Oh you're all fools

He assumes he is intelligent
No, he is dumb
He wants to pull the trigger with his finger to his thumb
Why do you take the Mick
You make all us sick

You spoilt little brat
I compare you to a rat
You who won't make this change.

Nicholas Tofallis
Highlands School, London

Clean Water

The clean, fresh bottle of water
As clear as clear can be
It bobbles around and moves about
But you're not even a bit thirsty
You go for it anyway
The first drop is as refreshing as a cold
Sweep of wind on a hot summer's day
It slides down your throat as fresh as a flower
Yet what would it be like if you didn't have the power
To go home with nothing there
The only water full of dirt and despair
The horrid, grimy water
As dirty as can be
As dirty as dirty can be
It sits in it while staring back at me
Who would think that it could take someone's life?
It was full of disease, as harsh as a knife
Imagine a place with fresh, clean water
You could have it cold or you could have it hotter
My family would be here and the dirt would be gone
If only there was a place where I could have one little taste.

Olivia Sharpe (14)
Highlands School, London

World Problems

This world in which we live
Is ours to love and cherish
But we as humans seem intent
On letting our world perish

Slavery still exists today
In some parts of this land
Often witnessed from afar
No need to lend a hand

Disturbing acts of racism
Still happen every day
How can the colour of our skin
Make us act in certain ways?

As bullets fall on fighting men
Another one of us dies
Another family suffers heartbreak
And all there is left to do is cry

Contrasting lives of people
Who have money for flash cars
Compared to cultures with only dreams
Where water is so sparse

How can humans do this?
Where is our self-respect?
We should all work together
Our world, we should protect!

Juliet Taaffe
Highlands School, London

Gender

Gender and sex
Gender is different to sex
Two sexes
Hundreds of genders

He-him
She/her
They/them
Ze/zir

Pronouns matter
Male, female and everything in-between
Pronouns matter
To those who are human

John was born a she and now a he
Riley was born a her and is now a they
Anna was born a she and is still a she
Pronouns matter to all of them

So many genders
So many to be
So how can you assume
Which one corresponds to me?

I could be a gender
And not be male or female
I could be gender fluid
Where my gender changes every day

Every day forced into a skirt
Or a dress
Every day forced into my sex
Not my gender
When all I want to be
Is human.

Thea Haines
Highlands School, London

Carrying Your Prison With You

It lurks in the dark
Or under your bed
In the corners of your room
And in your head

The monsters in your mind
Created by your fear
Creeping ever closer
They're getting very near

You'll never be free
They're always behind
You're never alone
When your prison's in your mind

We'll never let you go
We have you trapped
If you try to run
We'll always be at your back

If you want to escape
There's one thing you need to do
If you end yourself
You'll end us too

Stop us following
And keep us quiet
Do one simple thing
It'll make us silent

We lurk in the dark corners of your head
Wouldn't you rather be alone instead?

Ayse Orhan-Pennell (13)
Highlands School, London

A Tree's Life

I'm falling, turning, spiralling
Until I hit the ground
I did not fly and there I die
Until I am reborn

My mother is as tall as a skyscraper
Her arms hold my brothers and me
Until the time comes
We will hold our heads high
And then be battered to the ground

We are quite green as a family
We stick together, we do
Until a guy with a chainsaw and knife
Made me wish my children were free

And now here we lay together
In a line, side by side
Being taken from our home
We are all alone
On a rickety, slow truck ride

We make it to our final destination
We are taken by force inside
Our trunks are split down the middle
And ripped open from the inside

A tree's life.

George Athanasiou (13)
Highlands School, London

Untitled

Everybody in this world
Is born with a voice that could be heard
Everybody has something more to give, to cherish
To nurture, to love and inspire
But sometimes they ignore the ones that they hate
They torture
They keep to the rules that they learnt as children
Decisions, most don't understand all the torture
I thought there was more to life
Why can't love just take over and end all this madness?
I've had enough of seeing fear and the sadness
Religions and races that make you be you
I hope one day I won't need to say what I've said
So I guess this is my final prayer to the angels up there
I hope you're aware of what's happening down here
With my final tear for all of the people who lost their voice
To the madness of Earth.

Owen Edwards
Highlands School, London

Orphan

Dropped off at a doorstep in the pouring rain
Unwanted and alone, not feeling my mother's pain
Door opening slowly, waking me up
A kind-faced woman sipping her cup
Although weeping, now felt safe in her arms
But yesterday in a car seat playing with mother's charms
She didn't seem herself
Packing all the books away from the highest shelf
Old women came in surprised, then suddenly realised
My mother pleaded guilty, pleading for to me stay
But the old woman shouted, 'Who is gonna pay?'
I lay in my crib sound asleep
With a new home, where has Mother gone?
I wish I would have known
Dropped off at a doorstep in the pouring rain
Unwanted and alone, not feeling my mother's pain.

Holly Tyrrell (14)
Highlands School, London

Society

Society
In which teenagers find peace in suicide
Where the long lived slowly see everything crumble around them
When everyone's scrutinised and we give a round of applause for those who survive
Because once we hurt, it's hard to overcome

Society
In which our sorrows restrain
The depravity of it all
And so someone drinks to feel pure joy
For ignorance is bliss
But that's just because of the anguish of it all

Society
In which the word is misconceived
The ordeal of it all
And even though the screams of pain reverberate
There's just silence that greets us

Society
It's what makes us who we are
And we are what makes society.

Raqiya Cali
Highlands School, London

Beauty

She sat staring at her reflection
No friends could give her protection
From society's cruel standards of what is beauty
Tears rolled down her cheek
The standards she would never meet
In her eyes no make-up could cover her cries
She looked at every flaw
As she wanted to fix it more and more
Alone she would not condone herself from finding peace
As she felt the urge to cease to exist
She did not realise beauty is from within
Not seeing her pain was our greatest sin
We all now have to live without her and her beauty, that is true
We watched her as she grew but she flew
To a place far away, much to our dismay
Her pain has left but so has she
Drowning in regrets we all shall be.

Hannah Porter (14)
Highlands School, London

Separate But Equal

Separate but equal
That's what they are
One has a bicycle
The other has a car

Their lives are so different
Just because of one thing
One has black skin
The other has white

One can never get a job
Because of his skin
The other always gets a job
No matter what it's in

One has a single mattress
Lying on the ground
The other an apartment
Thirty stories up, in the clouds

Separate but equal
That's what they're not
One lives in poverty
The other does not

But they could change all this
That's what they don't see
If it weren't for the horrible
Racist society.

Jack Dewhirst (13)
Highlands School, London

Technology Is Taking Over

Humanity
It's driven by technology
Every app you use
Every game you play
It seems to wash the great memories away

The times have changed
It's all about devices when it should be about
fun and games
All the tweets you post
All the text messages you send
They cause gaps in relationships that aren't easy to mend

Haters hide behind technology
Instead of fighting for equality
Staring at a screen
It corrupts your brain
Reading comments full of hatred can cause you to
think the same

Humanity
It's driven by technology
Every app you use
Every game you play
It seems to wash the good memories away.

Shobhana Singarayer
Highlands School, London

Night

The night is dark.
The silence is deep.
I stand alone,
In the shadows of light

The moon so bright,
as white as snow.
Its gaze is pallid and ghastly,
It's almost as if the moon has a million stories
Stories of twinkling stars, snow and ice and mysteries of the universe from day till night.

I can hear an owlet's hoot
The silence still here.
The sound of crickets is something,
I cannot bare.

As I breathe in the misty night air
I imagine and realise that nights are filled with endless, endless weeps...
And endless cries and broken hearts, every time
Every night is sad and different, yet every night's...
The same.

Zara Satti
Highlands School, London

If You Could Change Anything

If you could change anything, what would it be?
For me, it'd be how we see equality
We are judged in life by the colour of our skin
While many of us are tortured within

People are racist, even to this day
The weak ones like us just walk away
It is said that beauty is skin deep
Yet many are still scared and still weep

Why do we blame one race?
For the problems another will not face
But we still judge one another
Based solely on skin colour

If only we weren't so critically scathing
Imagine how much easier life would've been
If you could change anything what would it be?
For me it'd be how we see equality.

Ashni Backory
Highlands School, London

Your Dove

I know life can be beautiful
It can be sad
Sometimes people around you are mad
But think of life as a dove
Love

A bird that is there
That doesn't go away
So it reminds you that sometimes life isn't fair
But life doesn't go your way
Think of a dove in the sky above

Though if life is going well
Just enjoy it while it lasts before it leaves your sight
As all things can come crashing down
Just be quick as it can happen in one night
Think of the dove in the sky above

But when you are home
After a tough day
Spend the time
With the family who love you
Think of your dove in the sky above.

Evan Eldridge
Highlands School, London

Beauty

She was so insecure
She was so ashamed
Everyone saw her differently
When underneath she was the same

To her, the world was cruel
Full of judgement and hate
Anywhere she went eyes followed
All because of some weight

The time they waste on shaming others
They could've spent on making themselves
So they too could have beauty
Not only outside but inside too

For some, life just gets too much
Thanks for all those who are full of anger
She didn't make it through the shaming
But the guilt left a voice in each mind
Of those who denied the world of this girl
Everyone is beautiful; never forget it.

Charlotte Dodd
Highlands School, London

The Refugee

I run with a sack in my hand
And blisters on my feet
With hopes in my mind
And dreams of all kinds

The sun beats my neck
The sand burns my toes
My thoughts filled with dread
But that's all in my head

I dream of a house, a garden
And plentiful food
I dream of clothes, a wardrobe
And nice, new shoes

Sometimes I cry with nothing to eat
Sometimes I weep with a chill in my feet
Sometimes I sob with nothing for cover
Most days I dream of good days to come

I hope to be strong one day
With nice words to say
But for now I dream
And that's just me, the refugee.

Hala Abughazza
Highlands School, London

Siblings

When I was just me
I could play all day
And sleep all night
Just me until I turned three

It was my sister and me
My new toy
The one who was always there to
Widen the branches of our family tree

Then two became four
Best friends one minute
Deadly enemies the next
A constant knock at my bedroom door

All I want is silence
To get me away from all this madness
You little tyrants
Please just stop being so defiant

But in the end I would've been lonely
Without my siblings to look after
Always someone to interrupt my answer
I'm glad it's not just me.

Grace Kent
Highlands School, London

What Is This World?

Why in this world are we all accused with false accusations?
Why is it still believed that women can't rule a nation?
Why is it still assumed that men are women's salvations?
When are we going to end this invasion?

This world is full of way too many connotations
Where thousands of people face discrimination
Where women are 'weak' and men are 'strong'
Where straight is 'right' and gay is 'wrong'

Where children spend all day staring at a wall
Where police are busy call after call
Where you're judged whether you're short or tall
Why can't this end once and for all?

Moneera Ali (14)
Highlands School, London

The Voodoo Doll

I've got pins in me, pins in me
I'm being controlled, set me free
From this shallow prison encaging me
You zip my mouth when I want to say
'I'm gay, I'm gay, don't take me away.'
I'm breaking free, I'm breaking free
Now I can be me. I've tumbled out
So hard and loud, but now I'm free
Don't stay away from me.
Yes, I'm gay now you know it's true, stop treating me like I'm nothing to you
I've told you now, so leave me be, as I can't stand you hating me.
You can't control me, I'm not your voodoo doll,
I've cut the strings I'm shiny, new, gold.

Marley-Marie Stewart (13)
Highlands School, London

Our Generation

Fake friends:
You know she's a fake
And you just can't work out why
And when she says, 'We're friends,'
You know it's just a lie...
Our generation.

Boys:
The guy says, 'I love you.'
You believe it's true
But then he walks out the door
And says, 'To hell with you...'
Our generation.

A girl's mind:
Perfect clothes, perfect hair
Perfect make-up, perfect perfume in the air...
Our generation.

Racism:
Black is black
White is white
Life is always
A racial fight...
Our generation.

Frankie Merrick (14)
Highlands School, London

You Were There

You were there
The day I entered this world
You were there
I took my first steps
You were there
I learned how to tie my laces
You were there
I can ride a bike now
You were there
But some things have to change
In a heartbeat or a blink of an eye
Everything has changed
I live a different life
On 17th of September 2008
You weren't there
It's my birthday
You weren't there, but you know
I started secondary school today
You weren't there, but you know
Because even though you weren't there
I know you can see me
You're always there.

Caitlin Flanagan
Highlands School, London

Glasses

They say if you wear glasses
You're considered a nerd
Small and inconsiderable
Lonely and without a herd

But if you stop and think
It'll be you that'll sink
And drown in your thoughts
While you type in ones and noughts

All of these computers started killing your eyes
And you carried on eating burgers and fries
But when you had your test
Your hate started to rest

That's when you became one of them

They say if you wear glasses
You're considered a nerd
But in the end
You are gonna be heard.

Dogus Grosu (13)
Highlands School, London

Will She Ever Be Happy?

Looking at the mirror for hours on end
Hoping and praying her life would amend
Ugly, horrible, stupid too
The only words she ever knew

Peering around her empty room
Filled with sadness and lots of gloom
Her life was slowly slipping away
Very slowly drifting astray
No one knew, no one cared
All alone she simply stared
Into a place she'd never seen
All lovely, fresh and very green

Then she blinked and was back again
Back into this place
She can't escape
Full of black holes and many dead ends
All she longed for was a friend.

Megan Bicknell (13)
Highlands School, London

Flame

A flicker in the dark, a bright, but righteous spark
A decisive dictatorship, controlling every relationship
All that my group and I stand for, is unfairly considered against the law
Hangings in the street, whipping at their feet
This fire won't go out, though just a flicker it may be
Staring through the flames, to spot something you can't see
We stand with one another and march onwards together
This fire won't go out, though just a flicker it may be
They work hard to blow out our flames, but can't seem to get us tame
A flicker in the dark, a bright, but righteous spark.

Baysu Kurt (14)
Highlands School, London

Life

What is life, why is it that we are born?
Does it just lead to death, or something more?
Some people say it has no meaning
Others say it is something to believe in

Everyone has their ups and downs
However, we should never give up and work our way around
We should not dwell in the past
Instead live in the moment as long as it lasts

Seven billion people in the world and the population continues to grow
New life, death, that's just how it goes
So what is life and why is it that we are born?
Does it just lead to death or is there something more?

Khushi Khatry
Highlands School, London

At The Ranch

Here I am outside
Just like the outsiders
Every day different routine
Treated differently just like mice
Taken away from my identity
Which hurts me, hurts me
On the ranch, sitting on the huge, strong branch
Just like a dog waiting for instructions to be told
I'm always in different places, been sold by different men
Never a day when the sun shines on me
Stuck in the bunkhouse, seems like a prison
It doesn't seem like home
We sleep on foam
In the 1930s I'm thirty
Need to go, instructions waiting for me
Trauma, trauma.

Sifa Sahiner (13)
Highlands School, London

Bananas

Bananas, bananas
They always change
Some people think it is very strange
But actually humans are exactly the same
Being different all the time like it's some sort of game

Bananas, bananas
They start off green
Just like a human turns into a teen
Yellow is the next colour the bananas go
Just when a human thinks the days are going slow

Bananas, bananas
They finally turn brown
Just as a human leaves their home town
The human gets on with their own life
While the banana is eaten and cut with a knife.

Owen Sinclair Jones (13)
Highlands School, London

Why?

Why am I sitting here thinking, *Why?*
Why am I here?
Why do I try?
Why do I cry at the things that make me who I am?
Who am I?
Will I always be like this?
Sad, distant, trying but never accepted
Drowning in a world of words and false hope
Some don't feel real, some don't have to feel the pain of the day
Some people don't have to try
Some people never wonder why
Some of us do amazing things without having to try
But some of us cry
Some of us get a bit of blood on our hands
Some of us are human.

Mia Arney (13)
Highlands School, London

What Is This World?

What is this world?
Where girls sit staring at photos on Instagram
Thinking that they need to look a certain way
Where boys feel they have to be 'hard' to fit in
Where people are judged by the colour of their skin
What is this world where people are scared to go outside
Fearing they could be shot or abducted by a clown
Where gay is wrong and straight is right
Where the bombs in Syria are no longer a fright
We were all born free, yet we're taken away by the hatred that we see every day
What is this world?

Rianna Biswas (14)
Highlands School, London

Christmas

It's the time of year when family comes together
There's an atmosphere of joy; you wish it would last forever
Around the table we sit and chat
It's not an issue, just all the bright, white lights
Dancing across the room
We move to the decorated tree and open all wants and not necessities
I won't see some of these family members for a while
I'll miss them and can pick up the phone to call
But it will be a year till we sit at the table together again
So cherish those moments and never say never.

Olivia Koublis-Hakki
Highlands School, London

Imperfections

Why, when we look at ourselves, do we only see
our imperfections?
Yet when we look at another we see their perfections?

See, the way we think of ourselves turns into the way we
think of others
The way we think of others turns into the way we act
The way we act turns into what we become

Imagine you looked exactly how you wanted to
Would our society be better? This shouldn't do

Don't let our imperfections conceal our identity
When we interact with others let it be in sanity.

Naomi Leighton (13)
Highlands School, London

Arsenal

Every year is our year, but instead
We live with reality as
Every year we disappear and
Next year we get a guarantee

Arsene Wenger, the man of lies
Every year a new disguise
With another compromise
And next season likewise

However, on the contrary
Top of the league by February
But it is only temporary
And soon we are unnecessary

Battling for fourth by May
And for fans our last day
As Arsene Wenger runs away
It seems next season will be a replay.

Emre Dixon (13)
Highlands School, London

My Friend

Dear friend, here we are again,

Remember when we used to pretend,
Pretend how you were in charge,
But now I see you have no regard,
About our relationship as friends,
I can see in your face, you want it to end

I don't know what I have done,
But now I see I have been shunned,
So I'll take my things and leave,
Hopefully so I can let you breathe

But don't worry dear friend,
I plan eventually we can make amends,
And hopefully meet again.

Chinwe Opurum-Kpandi (13)
Highlands School, London

The World Today...

When we think of the world today what do we really see?
We see a world full of hatred and that's how it seems
We want to live in a fantasy - a really big dream
But really this is reality and there are no sun beams
Everyone wants power and riches because they're greedy
But no one really thinks about the poor and the needy
People shooting here and there
Not even thinking about who really cares
This is the world we live in - a world of despair
But when we come together, we will be prepared.

Nathaniel Angate (14)
Highlands School, London

Justice

He is my friend
He helps me through all my bad times
He helped me when I was being bullied
He was there for me
He will always be there

Justice

When I was down he brought me up
When I was sad he made me happy
When I was wrong he made me right
When I was angry he made me calm

Justice

When the world's falling apart
Or someone breaks your heart
There's only one person to save you

Justice.

Ryan McCowen
Highlands School, London

Trapped

Intelligence matters
Respect matters
But why does the colour of our skin?

Whether you're white or whether you're black
Somehow we still all face
Some type of mortal sin

Day in and day out
The same thing all the bloody time
Leave us alone
Leave us in peace and let us explore the beauty of life

Racism, racism, racism
You are evil and as sharp as a knife
Racism, racism, racism
You play with people's lives.

Katy Grande
Highlands School, London

Poetry Is Bad

I think all poems really suck
When I hear the word I want to run
Poetry is really bad
It's the opposite of fun

Why does it exist?
It gets worse with every rhyme
I think writing a poem
Is an unforgivable crime

Its the worst thing ever
Worse than the Cintendo Vii
There is no way of telling
How poetry scars me

I know it sounds hypocritical
But I had to explain this way
Poetry is evil
All poets, go away!

Miles Holder
Highlands School, London

Meth Death

They all say that an apple a day keeps the doctor away
But what really keeps the doctor at bay?
Here is the death of the boy on meth
He's only sixteen, his battle will begin
He's only sixteen, he cannot win
He had his first with his mate, Fred
He had his last on his death bed
He had ten a day and his life blew away
Like a leaf in the sky
That was his last day
That was the death of the boy on meth.

Alex Gendler Smith (14)
Highlands School, London

Untitled

I went home stoned
My mum clocked and moaned
She started to shout
Then I got kicked out
I caught the train
Got off at Camden and did it again
I got really high
Thought I was gonna die
It was fun at the time
Little did I know it was a crime
I saw the Feds
Thought I was dead
They took me away
Not to be seen another day
I was only sixteen
Fifteen years till I will be seen.

Mackenzie Joy (13)
Highlands School, London

Modern Day Gladiators

Racism is not a colour
Neither a race
All of our blood is the same
That runs deep within our veins

If we could lift up each other
And know that we all care
If we help our sisters and brothers
There's a bond that we'll share

On the streets
Chilling in the hood
We are gladiators
We must now, these days
Up all of our game.

Andre Charles
Highlands School, London

Untitled

I walk into the GP
Playing was a CD
The doctor calls to meet me

As frightened as I am
I have to be a man
And if all goes to plan
I will rejoin the clan

There in all their glory
The dead bodies lying gory

My scars can't be seen
But the pain is still there
Eagerly as I fight on
There is no more to spare.

David Kourides
Highlands School, London

Racism

Every day I get abused
Every day I get accused
I say equality for all
As it isn't even my fault
But still people do not care
They just stand there and stare
Whereas I think it is just unfair

They are always on my case
Because of my race
I can't get a job
Then I just sob
Just because of my race.

Henry Wackett (13)
Highlands School, London

Together

Together we stand, all on the same land
Blacks, whites, mixed and more
Catholics, atheists, Muslims on tour
Girls and boys, males and females
Who may have met over emails
Lesbians and gays, how they met might be a daze
Together we will build
All for one big shield
Together we will fight
All for one's rights.

Clare Hamid (13)
Highlands School, London

Untitled

As we dwell in the ruins
More are to come
We hear the sirens wailing
But there is nowhere to run
As they drop, the buildings shake
One by one they shake the Earth
Boom, death, *boom*, death
Screams are heard
As the booms are heard
Then there is silence
The innocent souls raised to Heaven.

Antony Patrick Milligan (13)
Highlands School, London

Justice

Our hero gives us justice
Our hero is our role-model
We look up to our hero

Justice describes our hero
Justice gives us hope
Justice is our hero

We believe in justice
Justice can come in many shapes and sizes
Justice is like an infection
It spreads all throughout society.

Kamoliddin Usman (13)
Highlands School, London

Racism

People get bullied because of their race
Equality for all
It's literally just a skin colour
Yet people don't care at all
Nelson Mandela, he saved mankind
He got sent to prison for a long time
He never gave up
Even though it could've cost him his life.

Eleni Petinou (14)
Highlands School, London

Anxiety

How do people walk down the street
not knowing if somebody
Is around the corner?
Or when you least expect someone to pounce?
Anything can happen at any time.
It's just a risk day to day we take.
Although nothing may happen, be wary - look
Left and right!

There are shops, cafes and bus stops nearby.
Even the faintest of footsteps can send
A chill up your spine.
The pipes are dripping and the gates are swinging.
Step after step, you start to realise...

Reaching the bottom of the street, all bones intact
The cold of the air starts to make the windows crackle.
The door opens steadily, letting out a painful screech and
Floorboards creak after creak after creak...

But there is light at the end of the
Hallway.
Spiders' webs are as bright as ever.
The stenching steam passes through your nose;
It is the smell of grape juice and blood.

The wind blows the door shut
And there is a noise upstairs.
It sounds kind of like footsteps but not
Mum or Dad's -
More like a shadow dragging a corpse across the floor.

The walls are closing in;
There's nowhere to hide
Apart from the charcoal oven that sits invitingly in the middle of the kitchen.
Trying to pull the oven door open,
The shaking makes the screws drop off
And the mouth of the oven eats me

Because I remove the trays and climb in.
Shadowy figures begin to appear on the wall.
They try to pull open the door
But you are hanging on for dear life -
The shadows will not win!

Sweat patches start to appear
And the screaming begins.
Pulling the door open, it is Mum and Dad -
In my head, the flesh is melting to the bone.

Nicholas Weatherhogg (13)
Islay High School, Isle Of Islay

Tribute To France

Blue, white and red
When you think of France you think of terror
Normal people with their lives shattered like glass
Unaware children, trying to make sense of their grieving country
Security are hawks watching every move, doing their duty for their country
Blue, white and red
People are trying to get on with their lives in a frightened country
People have rights which should be followed and obeyed
It takes a lot for children to understand what is destroying their country
Blue, white and red
Through French eyes gunfire is a noise of a predator screaming for prey
No one should have to hear that
The sky witnessed it all
Blue, white and red
The French are never going to give in, as long as the Eiffel Tower stands protecting its beautiful country
No matter what race, belief or gender, everyone is equal
No one should live in fear.

Sarah Eve MacPherson (12)
Islay High School, Isle Of Islay

Me And My Ducks

What kind of a person would have pet ducks?
A strange, weird girl would have ducks for pets.
Even though their home is far from deluxe,
The ducks run when they see my silhouette.
Hillary is slower than the runners.
The runners are less cute than the fat one.
Though she is much fatter than the others.
Though they all wiggle their bums when they run.
But apart from everything ducks are great.
The ducks always cheer me up when I'm sad,
The poo always smells despite what they ate.
But they always run when I'm mad.
When you see them you can't hold back a smile
I don't want them to go... not for a while.

Anwen Baker (13)
Islay High School, Isle Of Islay

A Sonnet For Island Life

Islay is the queen if the Hebrides
Play on the beaches and swim in the sea
Ride the ferries over the stunning seas
Isle of Islay is lovely I agree!
Taste some whisky at the distilleries
Sing and dance at the feis and festival
Islay has a lot of great history
The summer skies go an aestival-blue
But sometimes you feel cut off from the world
Going to the city is exciting
Going shopping feels like it's a dream world
When in the mainland you can go sighting
Although it's good living in the highlands
You sometimes feel lonely on an island.

Emily Mackie (13)
Islay High School, Isle Of Islay

Our Greatest Gift

The enchanting sound of your endless notes
Swirl and dance around in this timeless space
Wordlessly, the stories of past and present float
To touch the soul in the deepest place

I find you in the crash of the waves
And the sighing of the windswept sand
In the whistling of the wind, in the mouths of caves
And the symphony I hear across this land

Music is in the air and in our hearts
It was our greatest gift right from the start.

Amy Want (13)
Islay High School, Isle Of Islay

Dear Future

Dear future, I'm sorry for leaving the world the way we did
We were too busy bombing ISIS to realise that the
ice is melting
What you know as the Amazon Desert, believe it or not
Used to be called the Amazon Rainforest
It used to be filled with trees and oh...
Wait, you won't know what trees are
Trees were amazing - they were literally the air we breathed
But we chopped them down and for that I am sorry.

Joseph Hamilton (11)
Islay High School, Isle Of Islay

My Beloved

Your blessed words are like a cure to every harm
that is created
Your love for us is like the ocean where its journey has
no ending
The amount of love you raised was to such an extent
Which made us feel adored
It caused such a sympathy in me
That many hearts are blind to see
That your character is more well known than the ones
above us
You held yourself up to help this nation
You have been firm and strong
Your life was spent like a roller coaster
Although most times went smooth
But through ups and downs you went around
Always keeping a smile on your face, not too big
nor too small
You spent your life in such a way where you are less
accountable for things
If you were here today, you would have caused such a
fragrance in the air
Your beauty is of endless thought
Although you were so simple and fair
You went through so much grief and pain
Which we can't just ignore
And so many hearts have followed your path to stand with
you in Heaven.

Asmaa Mohamed (13)
Jamea Al Kauthar, Lancaster

Broken...

Left alone on the streets
With nowhere to hide
Nowhere to run to
And no one by my side
My parents killed by soldiers
In front of my very eyes
My brother captured and taken prisoner
In my dreams I hear his cries
Left alone in my room
It was me the soldiers couldn't find
But they took away my family
The day still haunts my mind
So I was forced to leave the city
To my life, make a new start
But I'll never forget my family
That'll always be in my heart
Left alone in the present
While my past is dead
But the memories come back to me
And mess with my head
This is the life of an orphan child
With false hope and crushed dreams
But even though she's broken inside
Within she hides her screams

Left alone on the streets
With nowhere to hide
Nowhere to run to
And no one by my side.

Kareena Yasmin (13)
Jamea Al Kauthar, Lancaster

Friends

As much as we say we won't decay, the bomb went off a week ago
The grass we once walked on has gone grey
I've told you I'm sorry, I'm sorry for hurting you, I'm sorry for leaving you
I'm sorry for unintentionally, unknowingly, even unexpectedly hurting you
But you played my heart like a harp and you left a knife in my back
If you gave me just a little more time, I would've been there for you from dusk till dawn
But now when I think of you, I mourn
I mourn over how you broke me down little by little
I mourn over how dumb, stupid and naive I was not to see you for how you are
I mourn over the fact that my time was wasted with you, I can never get those minutes back
We said we will never decay
We said we will make it through together
But the bomb went off a week ago, and the grass we once walked on has gone grey.

Tayyibah Ahmed (13)
Jamea Al Kauthar, Lancaster

The Love For My Parents

Two very special people who live with me
My life would have been very tough without you
My freedom would have been very tough without you
My work would have been very tough without you
It is a very big honour to have you
My life would have been like a flower, dead without you
I'm here to say just like you love me, I love you
Maybe I haven't said that
But in my heart I do
How you supported me to work
I had to make you smile
I might have refused your chore
But you never refused the law
Maybe I might be far away from you
But you are in my heart for sure
Forgive me for what I have done
Forgive me when I didn't eat my bun
Always forgive me, Mum and Dad
Just forgive me please
Maybe I haven't been so good
But I promise to try and be good.

Halima Shazad Sadia (13)
Jamea Al Kauthar, Lancaster

Lucky Charms...

I miss you!
I can't see you every day
Due to living far away
Please come and visit soon
And I will be over the moon
I miss you!
I can't wait to come home
So I am not alone
And be hugged by your loving arms
You're just like my two lucky charms
I miss everything about you
From your love to your care
You were always there
I miss you
Because you have done so much for me
And the most I have done is made you both tea
I miss you, Mum and Dad
I can't wait to come home
So I am not alone
And be hugged by your beloved arms
The ones who help me when I was young
And put me to sleep when they sung
I wish I could see that smile one more time
Just to ensure that you are fine
I love you, Mum and Dad.

Aamna Nadeem Chouhdry (14)
Jamea Al Kauthar, Lancaster

I Don't Know If There's A Tomorrow

I don't know if there's a tomorrow
Could you give me more hope?
I don't know if I'm going to fall
Could you give me a rope?

My brother's dead
My uncle's a traitor
Everything was destroyed including my home
And now I have nowhere to roam

The troops are storming
Killing with no heart
There's bullets everywhere
Tearing lives apart

My heart is bursting
How merciless people can be
Torturing at such ease
How could they be so blind to see?

People crying on the street
Their hearts deep in sorrow
As I walk through the dust
I really don't know if there's a tomorrow.

Yumna Razick (13)
Jamea Al Kauthar, Lancaster

My Amazing Family

You bought me up since I was small
You cared for me and told me how to crawl
You never left a chance to make me smile
You were ready to do anything for me
Even if it was to walk a mile

I owe a lot to you all, I don't know how to repay
I am speechless, I don't know what to say
No matter what happened you never left my side
Even when I used to be mischievous
I used to run away and hide

So thank you for all you have done for me
For looking after me and letting me see
I didn't know what was going on
In this ever so mysterious place
All you wanted to see was a smile on my face!

Sumayya Ali (13)
Jamea Al Kauthar, Lancaster

Racism

Why so much hatred
To those who are broken
Why so much hatred
To those with a frown
Why so much hatred
To the people around?

Racism hurts
Way more than a dagger
It tears your heart
Just like a mere shredder

Being nice
Is what people want
And being just
Is the way to go

Racism is verbal
A verbal type of killing
It kills the heart
With just a bit of speaking

So before throwing comments
And being a bit judgemental
Always remember
It honestly makes people...
Very sentimental!

Ferdousi Yasmin (13)
Jamea Al Kauthar, Lancaster

Peace

No more wars, no more hatred
Or even the slightest bit of jealousy created
Forget, forgive, move on - be kind-hearted
That's the way to get peace started

It's not so easy, you can say that for sure
But looking at the results you'll want more and more
Love and harmony, you'll learn to share
The jewels you'll find are precious and rare

Families reunited, lost ones found
Of battles and arguments there is no sound
It's time to sit back and enjoy the happy day
For which you strived in many ways.

Fathima Mohamed Rila (13)
Jamea Al Kauthar, Lancaster

Time

Tick, tock, time goes by
I sit down in school and watch it fly
A second, a minute, an hour goes by
All in a blink of an eye
English, maths and science and other subjects too
There's always some type of work to do
I think of how to fit it all in
But then the next lesson starts to begin
Homework takes two to three hours
And I haven't even been to the showers
Mum tells me to fetch the groceries
Then to set up the cutlery
Then at the end of the day
I think about everything whilst I lay.

Amina Begum (13)
Jamea Al Kauthar, Lancaster

Helpless Syria

Mothers crazily cry
Thousands of people daily die
They all scream, 'Help'
Most of them yelp
Heavy bombs continuously fall
Building are destroyed whether small or tall
Everyone hides behind the piles of rubble
Knowing that there is bound to be trouble
Children wish they weren't ever alive
So they wouldn't have to see their parents
stabbed with knives
No one famous has the heart to end this tension
All they have to do is speak about it and mention.

Aamna Rehman (13)
Jamea Al Kauthar, Lancaster

My Mum

My mum is like a flower that never loses its fragrance
My mum is as sweet as a box of chocolates
My mum is like a teddy bear that will never leave me awake
My mum is like the sun, she shines in every way
She is like a star that gets brighter and brighter every day
I love my mum and that's all I need to say.

Mahima Begum (13)
Jamea Al Kauthar, Lancaster

Man And Beast

Christmas Day: everyone cheering, as they hear crackles of crispy skin
Blood filling the thick, diseased moist air
As the delicious specimen lies waiting
Fire burning into its loving heart

Yet these ravenous beasts
Unaware of the barbaric things that this devoted creature has endured
Knives delving into the soft, living skin
Piercing into the life and love of the beautiful beast

There is no difference between man and beast
There is only pain
Yet we skin their soft, thick fur
And now dead, but alive!

Who would even know we cared?
While we sit proudly, on top of our majestic throne
Sulking, cursing at our life
Yet, no care for the being of these magnificent creatures

Fed, bread and slaughtered, the meaning of their life?
Knives, cutting, cutting, cutting
Day after day, after day.

Niles Kinder (13)
Merchiston Castle School, Edinburgh

The Screen

Why do we play these violent games
That climb in our minds
And wreck our brains?

Why do we shoot and stab and kill
All the people that cross our paths
On the screen?

Why do we make these violent games
Which change the minds
Of our young men?

Why do we go further
And go outside...?

Why do we take a gun?
Who told you to do this?
The TV screen did.

Why do you walk to your school
And play the game with your friends?
Why do you play cops and robbers?
Why do you destroy your friends?

Why do you have blood on your hands?

You don't know.
Ask that TV screen what to do.
It will not tell you.
Game ended.

Johnnie Dodds (13)
Merchiston Castle School, Edinburgh

Saturday school

Saturday - it's the day of the dead
The morning when nobody moves
Apart from a certain Edinburgh postcode
Where action is at its best

We have no options

What happened to weekends?
We all need them
But our weekend doesn't arrive until Sunday -
A brief pause for breath before Monday

Double maths doesn't bode well...
An extra forty minutes of twiddling thumbs

Then the most horrible thing of all -
English
Not only English
But on a Saturday!

But enough about students, imagine how the staff feel!
Have some sympathy for them
Dragging themselves away from their families to come and teach

Us -
And on a Saturday!

Toby Gray (13)
Merchiston Castle School, Edinburgh

Pollution

Thousands of fish
Like shattered glass
Swimming in the abyss of blue.
Light shimmers from the world above
Like dancing angels.
The waves slowly rise and fall,
Seabirds diving to grab some fish
Taking them home to feed their young.
A giant, blue creature -
A great, blue whale -
Trapped in a coil of rope,
A deadly snake of plastic.
The whale is fighting.
It can't afford to lose
But the snake is too strong.
The whale lets loose, one final cry
Before falling still.
The snake has won
And the whale drifts into the abyss below.

Archie MacLean-Bristol (13)
Merchiston Castle School, Edinburgh

Seasons

Long days
Bright nights
Warmth and sun
Flowers
Green leaves
That's what spring brings.

Longer days
Brighter nights
Warmth and sun
Ice creams
BBQs
That's what summer brings.

Shorter days
Dark nights
Sun and trees
Golden leaves
Dead-looking trees
That's what autumn brings.

Darkest nights
Shortest days
Rain and snow
Snowballs
Snow angels
That's what winter brings.

Spring
Summer
Autumn
Winter
That's what they bring.

James Gilding (12)
Merchiston Castle School, Edinburgh

The Beasts Are Vulnerable As Well

Beasts hide behind the curtains
Slyly waiting for an age for the chance to pounce,
Spearheaded teeth sharp
And deadly.

The opportunity approaches:
Long talons seep into the spongy soil,
Thick muscles tense like a shock from lightning.

Grazing gazelles gallop through
The thicket of solidified grass.
Hairs on the beast's neck perk up promptly like soldiers.

Pain shot through the body.
Red liquid poured out of the wound.
Movement and pain stopped.
Stillness filled the area with a feel of emptiness -
Death.

Adam Leighton (14)
Merchiston Castle School, Edinburgh

Harambe

Innocent
No knowledge
Every day looked down at
Until the boy fell
It was confusion
What to do?
He took a step closer to the boy
And stared
Then even closer
He softly took his arm
A moment of shock hit the creature, forcing him to run

Forgetting he was holding the boy

People from above
Stared
Shouted
The creature may have looked big on the outside
But he was nervously tiny inside
Suddenly, he heard something click
What was it? he wondered -
Next thing we knew - he was dead...

Tom Channing (14)
Merchiston Castle School, Edinburgh

Why Do People Like The Colour Red?

Anger and bloodshed
Pain and toil
All wrapped up in
Red's oil.

And yet...
Still

People enjoy
Claiming that red
Stands ahoy

All colours beneath
Red is the best
Though every time
Red is shed
It always ends in death.

So don't you agree?
Why does humanity
Like the colour I despise?

I hope red leaves people's hearts
And minds.

Neil MacPherson (13)
Merchiston Castle School, Edinburgh

Vietnam

I see lines
Of soldiers with guns
Shooting people
Who are innocent.

I pace to the nearest bush
Sliding in the dirt
Avoiding to be shot.

Dry, thirsty, hungry
I want to chew survival.
I drink some water and I am relieved.
The planes are like birds in the sky.
I see blood and I know -
I am already dead.

Ocean Nash (11)
Merchiston Castle School, Edinburgh

Do We Like Poetry?

Do we like poetry?
Ask yourself, think...
Do you... does anyone?
Have you got an answer yet?
What is it, what was that?
No
Of course it was...

Tom Logan (13)
Merchiston Castle School, Edinburgh

Roof Wonderer

Up here the stars felt so near
It was like I could almost reach out and touch them
The air was thin and the night was silent
I could see just as well as I could hear

As the wind rushed past my hair
I realised all my burdens
I watched them glide away
They had been all I could bear

Every house was still
Not even a mouse could be heard
I cried out
The air had taken a sudden chill

I let go
My imagination had run wild
I tensed my muscles and forced my eyes open
Not every night was such a mesmerising show

Every night I sit here and view
Every night fly by
My life is a mystery
I'm a roof wonderer through and through.

Ruthie Quinn (11)
Oaklands Catholic School & Sixth Form College, Waterlooville

A Seed To A Tree

A seed is planted in the garden;
It grows and grows and grows...
But this plant has a story;
That flows and flows and flows...

A family tree is rising
The beginning of new life
A man has found someone
And this someone is his wife

A seed is planted in the garden;
It grows and grows and grows...
But this plant has a story;
That flows and flows and flows...

The couple have had children
Six to be exact
The children adore their parents
And they're adored back

A seed is planted in the garden;
It grows and grows and grows...
But this plant has a story;
That flows and flows and flows...

The children are now adults
They've found a place to live
Some have just got married
But some think love's a sieve

A seed is planted in the garden;
It grows and grows and grows...
But this plant has a story;
That flows and flows and flows...

The adults will be parents
But half don't want to be
The couple are delighted
For their children's news of glee

A seed is planted in the garden;
It grows and grows and grows...
But this plant has a story;
That flows and flows and flows...

The first child has been born
He has his father's eyes
Then Grandma and her husband
Hear the baby's cries

A seed is planted in the garden;
It grows and grows and grows...
But this plant has a story;
That flows and flows and flows...

Three more have been born
One boy and two girls
The parents and uncles and aunties
Treat their babies like pearls

A seed is planted in the garden;
It grows and grows and grows...
But this plant has a story;
That flows and flows and flows...

The brothers and sisters and cousins
And all the parents have come
To see the old couples' funeral
After all the work they'd done

A seed is planted in the garden;
It grows and grows and grows...
But this plant has a story;
That flows and flows and flows...

And there the story continues
With mysteries and sadness and mirth
The family tree has millions
Of people and deaths and births

A seed was planted in the garden;
It grew and grew and grew...
But this plant had a story;
That flew and flew and flew...

Grace Lewis (12)
St Benedict's Catholic College, Colchester

My Days

Waking up, feeling a fright
Didn't have a second of sleep last night...
Face is pale, feel constantly sick -
I'm sure this bully thinks I'm thick!
I try to resist but just can't ignore
When I'm at school there will be more and more!
Step in the gate; my eyes starting to stare
This is the start of my constant nightmare
Wish I was different, someone who's cool
Dreaming of an easy life, when I'm at school
The bells rings, I tiptoe out to break
They attack me like a lion eating a steak!
Punched, kicked, all happens to me -
If you could hear, you would soon see
Break ends and I'm in tears

How long will it last - days, weeks, years?
Hurt, cut, bruised, bleeding
The bullies are all slowly succeeding
Limp back to class, won't make a scene
Sit at the back, why are bullies so mean?
Shivering with fear, just can't tell:
I'm now in the living hell
School ends, I run out the gate
I have to go, before it's too late!
If I dared it would just get worse
Why me? Am I under a curse?

Rijin Thomas Rajan (11)
St Benedict's Catholic College, Colchester

The Monster Inside Me

Deep within the shadows I creep
Is there something that I seek?
To find a reason why I live
For in fear of death, it's death I give

Anyone who crosses my way
Won't live to see another day
As long as there are people to kill
The world is completely at my will

Is it me or is it you?
Try to see this from my point of view
Full of bloodlust, full of hate
I never had a choice in fate

Is this darkness, or is it light?
Who can teach me wrong from right?
I'm invincible, with power over sand
You'll know it's the end when I reach out my hand

I'm the Angel of Death so you'd better watch out
I'll kill you all, without a doubt
What can save me from this life I dread?
It's the word - that's been scarred on my head

This loneliness that eats me inside
These horror-filled fears that I try to hide
Now the whole world can read what I lost
I was made a weapon and my life was the cost

I love no one and fight for me only
You wouldn't understand, you've never been lonely
Shunned by everyone and feeling this pain
Now do you understand why I'm insane?

Surrounded by darkness, nowhere to hide
If I fall asleep, I'll be eaten from inside
This demon is restless, its presence I dread
Every full moon it must be fed

Your blood will make for a tasty meal
Is this true aliveness I feel?
Something is missing, something's not right
How could I have lost this fight?

Am I just like him, and him like me?
Is there something that I can't see?
Why can't I see it? It's very clear
It's only the feeling of loneliness I fear

Is there truly a lesson to learn?
I think my life is in for a turn
For better or worse? I may never know
But I'll have to accept that what will come will go

Confusion is suffocating me, I'm up to my head
If this keeps up, I might as well be dead
A new reason to live? What might that be?
I'm so tired, so we'll just have to see...

Natasha Gail Escabarte (13)
St Benedict's Catholic College, Colchester

Compulsory Asylums

I'm insane
Don't worry, I'm not trying to act shifty
But I would be nuts if it were 1950
I walk down corridors that promise education
But instead deliver anxiety, torment and humiliation
You wouldn't guess that this is an asylum
Well, that's because it insists on being silent
And denies and crime committed
That it's only a matter of time
Before we're grateful for what they've done to us

I guess I should be

How can I forget the days
When those doctors used their blade
Like words to damage my self-esteem
But still claim that we're all on the same team?
I'll never forget the focus on maths and arithmetic
And the excluded advice on how to balance a cheque book

I'll never forget the so-called lessons
That felt like therapy sessions
Because thank God I understand punctuality
But struggled discovering my sexuality
And my personality, there's no practicality
To my teenhood because it's
Steeped in formality

The mitochondria are the powerhouse of the cell
Info like that resembles a bell
Constantly ringing in my head
Because if I fail these exams I'm dead
We study books from hundreds of years ago
But forget about the highs and lows
Of mental health because what could be more
Important than the wealth of
Knowledge, we'll definitely need for the future?

I wonder if I'm crazy or if the system is
Because we aren't educated on LGBT
Along with our ABCDs
Despite the fact that it should be normalised
And not formalised
There are children killing themselves because they think
They aren't good enough, there's a link
Between what they were taught
And what they thought
About themselves

I cannot comprehend that you believe that this evidence
Shows no relevance
It does

Students in compulsory asylums that are called schools
Have the same stress levels as mental patients
From the 1950s
I dare you, tell me it's the kids' fault.

Gareth Moriarty
St Benedict's Catholic College, Colchester

Natural

'It's natural,' they said
They're made completely of plastic
They tell you that all of it's real
Not about the years of blood, pain and tears
And not eating a single meal

'It's natural,' they said
the people you watch on the TV
With smiles to dazzle the blind
Block out their flaws with needles
And sculpt their faces with knives

'It's natural,' they said
The physically perfect people
Who never seem to be ill
Have dark, sleepless nights and anxiety frights
Over the growing surgery bills

'It's natural,' she said
You think she's perfect don't you?
The model who just walked past
But you don't see the beauty hidden
By her vibrant, colourful mask

'It's natural,' she said
But she drowns her hair in buckets of bleach
She covers up her face
She replaces her imperfections at a very urgent pace

'It's natural,' she said
Her skin turns all one colour
Her eyes from brown to blue
Her sloped nose slims and straightens out
Her hair looks glossy and new

Under all the camouflage
Under the war paint
Is a sensitive, fragile creature
Who's both a devil and a saint

That everyone is a human
They stand up proud and tall
But at a single, tiny word
They crumple, down they fall

Pain is beauty?
No

Beauty is the scars on your forehead
The birthmark on your knee
It's friends that come and friends that go and
Friends that never leave

It's figuring out a plan
Discovering something new
Doing something amazing that you
Didn't know you could do

Beauty is confidence and happiness...
Not just a pretty face
It's natural.

Orla Gosling-Campbell (12)
St Benedict's Catholic College, Colchester

My Poem

It was an early morning, a cold, early morning
The wind moving to place, place after place
There was a small house in the middle of an
Ordinary street and I was in it

I cried in it
I felt like nothing meant anything to me any more
I felt dull in it
I felt angry in it
I felt mixed feelings about things I didn't know I was thinking in it
But I knew that I could never see her any more, anywhere

A patient lost a battle against cancer
To me this is the worst day of my life
The worst day of my life I can think of
That day was the worst day of my life

A sad week later I was in a church sitting on the back bench
On my own, sitting on a bench
I cried so much that I felt like crying an ocean of water
I wish she could come back to me
Speaking those deep conversations we used to have
Watching me and my nan's favourite movie

Two years have gone past and I still think of you
Every night I still think of you.

Luc Hémeury (12)
St Benedict's Catholic College, Colchester

Pretty Colours

Being me is kind of hard,
I feel as if all around me, there are daggers in the ground,
I live a double life inside, a life where I strive for more.
Sometimes I look outside the window, and think:
Why do I bother? Why do I try?
Sometimes I just feel like running outside,
To the tall trees by the river,
The craft shop with the pretty pots of glitter,
The bakery that always seems to smell like sugar,
The iridescent night that yearns for company,
The feeling of pure joy, that I will never forget,
and the farmer's land, that sunshine seems to always
hit the brightest.
Sometimes I just want to wallow around and
forget my sorrows.

I know I want to lead an ambitious life I will not regret,
where the spices are spicy,
where the colour in the streets alone bewilder me,
where the clouds in the sky make indescribable shapes
and remind me of beautiful paintings, made by artists years
and years ago.
Where everyone accepts everyone, and we break bread
together as a world.
But now all I ask myself is, where did all the wonder go?
Since when did the children cry as their mothers
had to watch?

Since where did the negativity, war and destruction begin?
When did we start killing innocent lives?
When did we lose our humanity

I sit, and look out of the window day after day.
Night after night, just thinking:
Poems are thoughts, and thoughts are revolutionary,
emotions can be powerful, emotions can change a dynasty.
The more we speak the more we move, the more we move,
the more we can expect change.
It's depressing really.
Sometimes you want something so much, you are consumed by it
People depend on you.

Benita Mehri (12)
St Benedict's Catholic College, Colchester

A Mind War

Depression
It's a war
But it's against yourself
You can either win
Or die trying...
Your biggest weapon is your mind
And that's what you're being put against
Depression is a thief
It robs you of your happiness
You're dead inside
You are unaware of what's going on
It's a nightmare
Waking up in hell every morning
Knowing you can't change it
Knowing this is it
The voices get louder
The times get harder
You don't see a point in living
You're afraid of living
It's a ocean of fear
An ocean of emotion
You're always feeling more than one
You're never just happy
You're never too sad
You're just complicated
You feel too much

You can't help the tears
You're submerged in the ocean of sadness
There's no way out
Your breathing gets heavier
It gets louder
The voices just don't stop
Never-ending pain
Never-ending struggles
There's no escape
It's a war
It's time to surrender
You died trying
But now your family are crying
It's a permanent solution
Of a temporary problem
Suicide doesn't take away the pain
It just gives it to someone else...

Anjelina Bown (13)
St Benedict's Catholic College, Colchester

Why Discriminate?

People always hatin' and judging me before they
even meet me
You say black lives matter but I don't see you doing
anything about it
Yet, time and time again, another one's been shot
It just hasn't sunk into people's heads that a black life has
been lost!
In America alone, so many have died
How long will it take before people realise the issue of
black lives?
Because colour changes everything - my views
and your dreams
Discrimination happens everywhere, it's just as it seems
But why do you wanna judge me 'cause of my skin?
I'll never know, do you even really know what goes on
deep within?
It doesn't matter if you're tall, small, black, Asian or other
ethnicities too
We all matter, it's about what we do about it
Otherwise, there ain't a way around it
So just remember to always have hope
'Cause that's the thing that will help you cope
And you don't have to change anything 'bout you
But let who you are sculpt you

And in the end, we only have each other, just me and you
So why discriminate
When we could all just be best mates?

Genevieve Wersong (14)
St Benedict's Catholic College, Colchester

If...

If you could stop the heartache
If you could stop the pains
If you could stop the flowing hate
And stop the prejudice strains

The world wouldn't be weeping
So love wouldn't be leaving
Its cultures wouldn't be hated
And their people not illuminated

In the end these are just ifs
Hike the mountain; don't remain stiff
Walk the road, climb the cliff
Engineer society's motif

But you can't stop the ache can you
And you can't cure the pain in you
The hate is pouring through you
And the prejudice streams from you

How can you stop something that hurts you?
How can you cure something that's inside you?
How can you contain something that devours you?
How can you end something that's bred in you?

An ant can control an army
A bird can feed a newcomer
An ape can protect a family
A person can welcome a stranger

If you can't start co-operation
If you can't start a reformation
If you can't stop this aggravation
There will be no stop to discrimination.

Inge-Maria C Botha (13)
St Benedict's Catholic College, Colchester

Self-Belief

I wipe the beads of sweat off my level forehead and sprint
Because to sprint is in my biological blueprint
All I wanna do is leave an imprint
Even though I may be skint
Ordinary not extraordinary
Yet I long to leave my mark, so I run
I run as one with everything around me
And I feel the sun pour its sunlight onto me
Then whilst I'm running the voices yell:
Run stronger
Strides longer
Run stronger
Strides longer
Run stronger
Strides longer!
However
If your mind weighs a ton
Then everything is undone
Because when you run
The race is already won
Before the sound of the gun
So always lighten your head
Release the stress you lock up there
With a de-cluttered mind
You'll no longer be defined
Nor will you be confined by your limitations

You won't just run, you'll fly
And the negative thoughts will die
Leaving you with only aspirations
That's how you find your sprint
To cross the mental finish line with a hint
Of self-belief.

Mia Andrea Patterson (14)
St Benedict's Catholic College, Colchester

Stuck In A Dream

Do you know what it's like
To get stuck in a dream?
Everything starts out all happy and jolly
Laying in the sun, licking a lolly.
Then all of a sudden
You're being chased by a creepy dolly!

Do you know what it's like
To get stuck in a dream?
Firstly, you start off at nursery,
Then you find yourself
At your wedding anniversary!
Having passed your life
Through lots of adversity!

Do you know what it's like
To get stuck in a dream?
When you're lying in bed
And the wind is howling.
And all you can hear
Is our pet dog growling.
You wonder and wonder what this thing could be,
Through a crack in the curtain,
It's a shadow of a tree.

Do you know what it's like
To be stuck in a dream?
Endless hours looking at the ceiling.
Whilst inside I am screaming and screaming.
I think I'm dreaming.
About zombies and mean things.
But actually
They're in my room
Screeching and screeching.

James Stirling (12)
St Benedict's Catholic College, Colchester

A Nobody...

Why me, what did I do?
The one who cared so desperately for you
I'm alone, stuck in this place, my head is turned
Tears streaming down my face
You called me ugly, annoying, fat
To me there's nothing worse than that
But you? You don't understand

I stopped looking for monsters under my bed
I hear them screaming inside my head
The tunnel is long, there is no end
Well at least there is inside my head
Can't see the light, I doubt it's there
It's this life I really can't bear
Just this pressure
This unbearable pain
More weight on my shoulders
Each day I gain

The scars of yesterday
Are still here today
Trust me when I say
They're not going away
Nobody noticed
Nobody cared
You're drowning in pain
You're alive but you're dead

It's easier saying, 'Don't worry, I'm fine.'
When really you're basically dying inside
Like a dark empty room
A room just for me.

Olivia Farry (13)
St Benedict's Catholic College, Colchester

Image Of Mankind

In a human what do you really see?
A body on the outside, but darkness beneath
Nothing else but negativity
The things that drive evil upwards, no brightness or creativity
Black and white roams the earth
But colour and creativity needs to be saved for what it's worth
When will these dark feelings end?
At the next turning
In a few miles, or do we let it keep on evolving?
Terrorists and murderers all over the news
Revenge
But what does that make you?
Now infected, not knowing what to do
As the disease of evil spreads all over you
Slowly turning the world black with hatred
But where is the colour
The light in our hearts
Trying to break out, so just give it a chance
Anger and depression isn't the way to go
It's not the real you
So don't give it a go
All that's wrong with the world
Is when we close our hearts

But when we let the brightness shine through
That's when the world begins to move
And the colour starts.

Tristan Louis Perera (13)
St Benedict's Catholic College, Colchester

The Dust Bowl

It was a horrible day when the dust bowl started
It forced the Midwest to be departed
It ruined millions of peoples' lives
Men and women lost their husbands and wives

Then came the poverty, starvation and theft
People stole so much, there was nothing left
Farmers abandoned their crops and land
When they saw the cloud of dust and sand

Everyone scrambled what they had
And moved west, tired and sad
California was their destination
The state of comfort and vacation

But very soon, California was full
They could not even squeeze in a bull
So they shut everyone out of the state
It was like they were shut behind an iron gate

So they were forced to work on ranches
Sowing crops and cutting branches
Whilst they worked, they thought and sighed
All of their dreams had all but died.

Tom Brown (14)
St Benedict's Catholic College, Colchester

Busta Rhyme - The Poet Within

My Favourite Thing!

Football is my favourite thing
Watch me run past everybody down the wing
No matter what, no matter where
Put the ball at my feet, I'll make you despair

Give me any team you like
The final result will always be delight
Not first but that's okay
Give me a shot, I'll put it away

Football is my cup of tea
My excitement, my life, my home forever will be
The journey starts with me at home
Playing FIFA, becoming a pro

Knuckleballs swaying from side to side
Wondering what way the keeper will dive
Shameful and embarrassing too
Especially when I nutmeg you

At night I sometimes dream of the picture of me holding the number nine
Scoring my first goal will be divine

Football is my favourite thing
Watch me run past everybody down the wing...

Harry Owen Thomas (12)
St Benedict's Catholic College, Colchester

Appreciate

Imagine it is a normal day that is going in a flash
You sit down at the table and see their head drops down with a smash
Just appreciate
You run and shout for help with horror on your face
The sight of an unconscious loved one is what you have to embrace
Just appreciate
They said he suffered from a serious stroke
You stand and see that no one spoke
Just appreciate
Staring ahead with pain in your heart whilst you watch them slowly die
You think to yourself that you didn't even have a chance to say goodbye
Just appreciate
Love the people who take time to love you
Otherwise you will feel depressed and blue
Just appreciate
Tell someone that you love them and just don't do it later and wait
You don't know the future and loving them later could just be too late
Just appreciate...

Ama Wellahewage (13)
St Benedict's Catholic College, Colchester

Why Don't They Listen?

Why don't they listen to what I have to say?
Am I an outcast from all of their conversations?
Why don't they listen to what I have to say?
Do they think I am wrong to have my own opinion?
Why don't they listen to what I have to say?
Or am I just by myself in the middle of an ocean?

Is it wrong that I think racism is bad?
Is it wrong that I think that trafficking is banned?
Do they understand me?
Or am I just abnormal?
Do they think the same?
Or do they just follow the leader?

So why don't they listen to what I have to say?
Is it because I'm different in my looks and my ways?
So why don't they listen to what I have to say?
Just because I'm different doesn't mean I should be left in my own alleyway.

Bandi Cserep (13)
St Benedict's Catholic College, Colchester

A Sailor's Letter

The letter dropped into the box much like her heart did when it came
She egged the knife through the seal
Reluctantly slipping out the paper
Gazing upon the swirls of ink

Thoughts rushed through her head
She read the writing on the page
Scanning every crevice of the swirls

The image of his hand sailing across the page
The pen like the anchor
The intention like the breeze that pushed him onwards

She treasured this thought, this letter, this day for soon after another letter came
As she read this letter tears trickled down her porcelain skin
Her bright china blue eyes turned red and bloodshot
Her long brown locks tumbling out of their pins, slumping round her waist

He was missing at sea. But was he dead or alive?

Lucy Lester (12)
St Benedict's Catholic College, Colchester

Dawn Of Hope

Beyond the black of the night
I can hide my soul from you
For this empty jar of hope
Carries no clean residue
The body that you see now
It is just a rented room
Sheltering the unshaped me
Produced from my mother's womb

Beneath the gleam of the stars
I can find my path to cheer
For this sealed padlock of faith
And locked sense of atmosphere
Waiting for a perfect storm
To release the liable noose
My confidence growing and
Personality induced

Behold the crack of the dawn
I have let myself roam free
For I've grown out these shackles
So the whole wide world can see
The body that you see now
May still be a rented room
But now I see the good times
Things will get positive... soon.

Julian Olivagi (13)
St Benedict's Catholic College, Colchester

I'm Alone In The Room

I'm alone in the room,
Until I realise that you are behind me,
A dark shape I see,
I move my hand and so does she,
She looks like me,
She acts like me,
She talks like me,
She is as dark as the darkest night,
Inside her she is as bright as the brightest light,
I scream!
I scream!
I scream!
My silent scream I hear,
As I feel help is near,
But my blood is frozen,
Suddenly, I don't feel chosen,
I look out the window,
The sun goes down,
She fades away,
I say goodbye to today,
My cold tear freezes on my cheek,
She taught me that I was not a freak,
She showed me my true light,
Now I can move on to things with great sight,
Thank you I say, thank you,
As my fear passes away.

Amisha Muhandiramge (12)
St Benedict's Catholic College, Colchester

To Wait For The Win

Running, jumping, spins, turns
The thought of mistakes makes my stomach churn
I tripped on the beam
I fell off the bar
The bruises on my arms
My legs have got scars

I'm not ready to compete
I need to warm up
All these other gymnasts
One's sure to win the cup
I see the flips
I see the twists
I just close my eyes and clench my fists

What if I get deductions?
From vault or floor
I might get a medal
I mean, my routines aren't that poor
I stare into space until my name is called out
There was all this excitement and now it's all doubt

The waiting is horrible
I just can't let my team down
And then I hear the words
I had won the crown...

Maddie Barrell (13)
St Benedict's Catholic College, Colchester

My Poem About Dennis

There's a boy called Dennis,
Who is a menace,
But he treasures tennis
In fact, Dennis playing tennis is like a holiday in Venice.

Whenever he sees a basket full of tennis balls
He imagines serving them so hard it would break a wall.
But Dennis spends most of his time in school
So he messes about in the school hall;
He wishes the hall was a tennis court
And he could get an epic tennis report.

Dennis playing tournaments
Is as special as my fossil ornaments!
He wishes he could play every day
Seeing as it's so fun to play
Especially at the start of May.
Every morning Dennis would say,
'I wish I could play every day
Especially at the start of May.'

Louis Gannon
St Benedict's Catholic College, Colchester

The Refugees

The tide brought a boat full of refugees
Leaving their homeland that's full of disease
Disease of genocide, murder and war
Unrecognisable from life before

Bravery abound, boats run aground
Other boats perish and innocent drown
For everybody that lands on the shore
Another lost in the ocean before

Bodies on the beach where onlookers stare;
Death in our midst we offer our prayer

The mercy of God so hard to conceive
When a mother has lost her babe at sea

Asylum seekers full of despair
Are met with prejudice and an aggressive glare

Food banks awaiting to offer hope
But the borders close...
And turn back the boats.

Meadow Giles (13)
St Benedict's Catholic College, Colchester

Goal

There was a kid called Natt, he played football
Natt was fat but he wasn't bad at football at all
Natt played for Colchester Villa
Natt was on the ball whilst his mum ate a vanilla ice cream that she got from the Co-op
Whilst Natt did a Ronaldo chop
Clatter, he was fouled
There was a little bit of chatter, that chatter turned into a fight
Which gave the parents a fright
Natt stepped up to take
Making sure he was awake
He ran towards the ball, kick
He put it away; he was floored
When his teammates celebrated with him
Because of the goal that he just scored
Natt ran up to the pole on the side of the pitch and waved at his mum
She was proud that he scored a goal.

Matthew Hull (12)
St Benedict's Catholic College, Colchester

The Golden Goal

I have been waiting for this moment since day one
And there is nothing that is going to ruin this fun
The feeling is electrifying
I feel like I am on the verge of dying
For there is nothing defying
From me trying

The game has tied one-one
And there is nothing holding me back
I feel my career had already begun
With my powerful kick I thwacked

The ball went flying
I gave it all I got
And the other team is sighing
Maybe they should've not thought of me as naught

This different feeling
I haven't felt in years
The crowd made me feel appealing
And happy after the tears.

Lyle Gabriel Miano (12)
St Benedict's Catholic College, Colchester

Suicide

Suicide is so sad, it takes people over the edge
So we need to all pledge
To help the bad thoughts inside their heads
Suicide, it's horrible and terrible
People are going home
Thinking the only way out is taking their own life
With a scythe, rope or even a knife
And this causes all sorts of strife
We need to help them, it is so sad
And so very bad
That people are throwing themselves over the
White Cliffs of Dover
And this is why suicide has to blow over
Turn over a new page to a bright world
And this is why people should not go towards the light
So suicide and bullying needs to stop now.

Thomas Cresswell (11)
St Benedict's Catholic College, Colchester

Alone

Do you ever feel alone?
Worn down to the bone
Lived a good life, had lots of fun
Spent many good days in the sun

These times are so cruel
Run the race, followed the rules
Won some races, lost some battles
Your worn-out body cracks and rattles

Now tired and rusty, it's hard to roam
Lost in the world, far from home
Your poor, old body has broken down
Friends are gone, no one's around

Your race is run, you're in low gear
Now without a doubt the end is clear
You do what you can, waiting till the day
Angels will come to show you the way.

Luke Campbell (13)
St Benedict's Catholic College, Colchester

Irish Dancing

Sore toes and blisters
Wigs and tiaras
Illuminated colours
Of divine dresses
Enchanted, extraordinary
From what you see!

Tap, bang, clipping, clapping
Reel
Slip jig
Heavy
Hornpipe

Hard work and effort
Softs and heavies
Unbelievable pictures
Uprising energy
Floating high
Transcendent!

Tap, bang, clipping clapping
Reel
Slip jig
Heavy
Hornpipe

Sweet smiles and chatters
Glows of gold
Waiting calmly
Winners radiant
Trophies held
Grinning!

Amaia Lilia Jane D'Souza (13)
St Benedict's Catholic College, Colchester

I Thought You Cared!

Being around you made me feel special
That joy in my heart disappeared when I left you
I loved you but you never really cared
You looked into my eyes and told me you would always be there

You were never there for me
When I needed you the most
When you came home you treated me like a ghost
I made my decision to leave you
I knew it was a right decision even though...

You chased after me
You screamed my name
You panicked eagerly thinking I really cared
You broke my heart, don't you get it!
I left you for good so forget it!

Daniella Obianuju Akpiama (13)
St Benedict's Catholic College, Colchester

Different Types Of Heroes

Heroes. Who are heroes?
Real-life heroes, comic book heroes
All different types of heroes

Big ones, strong ones
Fast ones, small ones
All different types of heroes

Hulk, Thor, Flash and more
Batman, Ant-Man and Aquaman
All different types of heroes

Mothers, brothers
Sisters, fathers
All different types of heroes

So, who are heroes?
Why, anyone you want!
Mothers, brothers
Sisters, brothers
Comic book characters
Real-life figures

All are different types of heroes.

Niamh Mary O'Neill (14)
St Benedict's Catholic College, Colchester

If

If I told you lies that I had to hide
Would you try and find out what haunts me inside?
If I told you I cry myself to sleep
Would you try and figure out what hurts so deep?
If I told you I had a hole in my heart
Would you have tried to heal it from the start?

If I told you I've been hurt too many times
Would you try and get what was originally mine?
If I told you that I had permanent scares
Would you tell me to look up to the stars?
If I told you I'd rather be dead
Would you tell me, 'I will love you instead?'
If...

Mya Obwoya (12)
St Benedict's Catholic College, Colchester

Brother

He doesn't feel it
He doesn't know
He tries so hard
But he just can't get the flow

The emotions are slurred
For you and me
You dear little boy
With a face so sweet

Fight for your life
Or flee into the night
You dear little boy
With a soul so milky white

It's hard to understand
Because the noise is so loud
You dear little boy
With knowledge so vast

But when you step into outside
You can see that he's trying
You dear little boy
My brother.

Abigail Rose Wetton (12)
St Benedict's Catholic College, Colchester

Darkness

It engulfs you from the inside out
A coat of blackness hides you out
A blanket of blood-curdling red grass
That cuts into your legs and leaves red marks
Criminals hide in the cover of the night
Days, nights and the years go by
And the days become night and more years go by
Giving the criminals more time to strike

Bang, bang goes the gun
You're lying in the sun
But the sun is none
Darkness is back, the fear starts to spread
The next minute is done and now you're dead...
Darkness, darkness.

Shania Hughes (12)
St Benedict's Catholic College, Colchester

In My Heart

In my heart you cannot see
It is too blurry to be beneath
There is only one thing that is so clear
There is something that I fear
To tell you that I'm always here
Even though I overhear
From my heart
This piece of art
Which is to declare
How much I care
Deeper, deeper, deeper
I might find my peace-keeper
Under the light where it may shine
There is a sign of it being mine
Chased until the ending where it is no more
Standing in front of me is what I have been looking for
But in my heart it all is...

Ore Ayanbadejo (12)
St Benedict's Catholic College, Colchester

Autumn's Falling

Crisp weather with swirling leaves, browns, reds and golds
Face against the cold glass
Thoughts of summer are old
Mornings and evenings are darker, the sparklers feel alive
Knocks on the door and children's chorus
Witches and ghouls are rife
Cosy blanket and crackling fires, chocolate and spices bring warmth
Curling together our scarves all wrapped, eager for the times ahead
Muddy paths, our Wellingtons on, snapping twigs and dodging webs
They lead us on a dance at twilight
For the stars to light the sky.

George Sibthorp (13)
St Benedict's Catholic College, Colchester

One Blank Sky

Staring out into the blank sky
Wide awake I lie
The tears roll softly down my face
Was I really made for this place?

Everything taken for granted
My views on the world are slanted
Restless eyes fighting to see
What this place is meant to be?

Sunlight softly dims
The dark water moonlight skims
Sore eyes withdrawn
Is there no coming of dawn?

East, west, north, south
Silently and still does sit my mouth
Darkness controls my sight
When will I see the light?

Freya Richardson (13)
St Benedict's Catholic College, Colchester

Journey

I've been around the world
Yet I feel that I have stayed in one place
Life is just a journey
There are bumps along the way

I have many homes
But I feel I don't belong in any
Life is just a journey
There are bumps along the way

I want to reach high
But people tell me I can't
Life is just a journey
There are bumps along the way

I've met new people
But I think the old ones are the best
Life is just a journey
There are bumps along the way.

Nicole Lentas (13)
St Benedict's Catholic College, Colchester

Books

Silly books, icky books
Books that are lost down the sofa
Books that you read over and over
Books that wake you up at night
Books that make you take flight
Books that you should buy today
Books that make you want to stay
And books that make you yell hooray!
Books that never seem to end
Your eyes will pop out as you discover the joys
you will uncover
But there are also books that make you weep and cry
And books that make you say goodbye
And now I have to fly, for now I have to say goodbye.

Mary Richardson (11)
St Benedict's Catholic College, Colchester

The Love Triangle

I wish she was mine
She's truly divine
Her eyes are shining bright
Her locks are yet to beat
I love her from her head to her feet

She is always with that other guy
If she was with me I could make her heart fly
It will go up and down and round and round
It will be such a sight
So much she wouldn't make a sound

My love for her grows more and more
Then my love for s'mores
If only she could see
It could be me...

Francesca Jacks (13)
St Benedict's Catholic College, Colchester

The Cup Game!

Today is the game
I will win
My team will win
I
Am put on as a substitute
I feel alone on my bench
I await for the gaffer to call me on the pitch
He eventually called me to come on
I thought to myself
This is my time
My team is drawing
I will score for us
Eighty-ninth minute
I'm on the ball
I'm through
It's just me against the goalkeeper
He comes out of goal
I chip it over him
Yesssss!

James Christopher Beattie (12)
St Benedict's Catholic College, Colchester

The Girl With A Lot Of Charm

She had a lot of charm
She didn't like the country
She had a charm
She had it in her arm
She hid behind the sun tree

The girl with a lot of charm
Was once thought of an a dummy
She eased my sore forearm
My sore, sore forearm
Then she fled away from me

I knew the girl with a lot of charm
Would always hurt me
The girl with a lot of charm
The girl with a lot of charm
Please don't ever hurt me.

Shalom Awesu (13)
St Benedict's Catholic College, Colchester

Inside!

There is a girl in the front of my class
Who just wants to smile and laugh
She draws pictures on her body
Her skin will open and red will show
She will cut, she hurts, she survived
She laughs, she cries, she died

Once she smiled
Once she laughed
Once she cried
Once she even wanted to die

She sat in her room
Falling to doom
Knowing she would die
She whispered,
'It kills me inside.'

Chardonnay Fuller (12)
St Benedict's Catholic College, Colchester

Bullying

Bullying is bad
It makes people sad
Dark shadows leaning over
Sometimes you just want to sit on the sofa
Late at night they hug their mums tight
They go home and take their life
With a knife, which is not alright
Now the bullies feel bad
And now they feel sad
And know what they've done
And realised it wasn't fun
No bullying is right
No bullying is nice
Instead of a knife
Look for the light.

Tilly Leach (11)
St Benedict's Catholic College, Colchester

The Small Scorer

Running down the wing
Looking like a king
About to cross the ball
But he was too tall

People shouting at me
Like I'm not the best

But inside I know
I'm better than the rest

It was near the end of the game
And I was feeling so ashamed
I got the ball

My fans were cheering
The opponents were fearing
I took the shot...
Yessss!

Manny Roarty (12)
St Benedict's Catholic College, Colchester

Lies...

He said to me,
'You're beautiful.'
Yet I look at myself
And say, how?
He looked at me in the eye
So I stared at him back

He took a deep breath
His eyes became bigger
And then he opened his mouth

I just can't stand that he is a fibber
He said he loved me
And then walked away
But I saw him with another girl the other day.

Lalea Garcia Radones (12)
St Benedict's Catholic College, Colchester

Bullying

It's bad
To be sad
In a school
With a fool
Who rules our class
Bullying me
He's tall with his ball
That he kicks around the school
He kicks it in my head
And calls me names
I go home
I go home to have my meal
As I feel the hurt
In my heart that I had another day
Of bullying
This will continue until...

Victoria Kessel (11)
St Benedict's Catholic College, Colchester

Anti-Bullying Poem

One word
Just call me nerd
Four-eyed freak or even geek
Punch me, hit me, make me scream
I just have one last dream
Call me a flea
Just leave me be
Why all this hate then call me mate?
When you lie it makes me cry
Spit, hit, I've had my last fit
My last word has been heard
Make a truce, stop the abuse.

Chloe Claxton (11)
St Benedict's Catholic College, Colchester

Help Me

Help me
I'm drowning
The blood pours from me and spreads into an ocean of crimson despair
Help me
It's crushing me
This growing weight on my shoulders
I slowly pinning me to the ground
Help me
I'm dying
Slowly but surely, the world begins to fade
Help me
Please.

Anna Kelpi (13)
St Benedict's Catholic College, Colchester

The Beach

On a hot, sunny day, on a hot, sunny beach
Sat a little girl called Penny Bleach
She liked to eat so she took a seat
And ate a peach

She could feel the heat coming towards her
So she stood up and said a speech
'Woah, what a heat on this sunny beach.'

Shanice Acheamponmah (11)
St Benedict's Catholic College, Colchester

Identity

Do you have an identity?
Is it still in your memory?
This isn't easy for me
I'm trying to write this so it fits in a melody
I'm trying to remember me
And if you still remember me
I'll wipe away your memory.

Jonpaul Fisher (13)
St Benedict's Catholic College, Colchester

The Soldier's Confession

I'm sitting in a room awaiting my death
I think this is going to be easier than fighting
I thought I could fight, I really did
But when time came to fight
Time stood still
I saw my best friends die in seconds by my side
Sergeant Major shouted, 'Go private, go!'
But I couldn't
So I did what cowards do, I ran back into the putrid trenches
I was scared, so scared
I saw good men die at my side
Men who thought they would be heroes
But these men won't even get a proper burial
They'll get piled up against other bodies
And the rats will get their dinner once more
These men tell me they see us winning the war
But I tell them honestly, 'No.'
British newspapers make up a bunch of baloney
Anything to get the public thinking we've only lost fifty thousand instead of a million
When I ran back Sergeant Major grabbed me into his office and said
'Boy, I don't want to do this but you'll get shot by nightfall.'
Here I am awaiting my death
Waiting to get blindfolded
Here I am awaiting a white piece of fabric to get attached to my heart

But will I get regret running?
Hell no, I won't
I won't be like those men with ripped out limbs and mustard gas eyes
I would rather die a cowardly death
'Left, right, left, right, left, halt!'
They're coming, my friends
And I can't stop them.

Eva Callaghan (14)
St Ronan's College, Lurgan

Our Girls

It has now been two years
Why haven't we got our girls back?
Their families are still choking on tears
Like a noose is tightening round their neck
We sit at home filled with relief
Rejoicing that we aren't victims of this war
Though isn't this just one idiotic belief
About these girls, that there won't be any more?
It shouldn't matter if there are ten less or ten more
They are brainwashed and hidden behind a
cold, unopening door
It should be the men who stole them, in a cage
that is bolted
The tears that they shed, the prayers that they call
Go unanswered; no one is looking at all
The screams of agony, the shrieks of pain
Wondering will they ever see freedom again?
We must do something before it's too late
Before another kidnapping, murder or rape
Remember those girls, each one younger than me
Imagine a life not knowing if you'll ever be free
Let's show them we care, that they aren't forgotten
Let's bring our girls home or in graves they'll be rotting
It's time to end the hurt, the agony, the misery
Get these girls home, leave the war in history.

Aoife Elliott (17)
St Ronan's College, Lurgan

The Gummy That Didn't Give Me A Sore Tummy

When I opened my bag of gummy bears
I was shocked to see what was sitting there
An ugly duckling if you like;
A gummy coloured grey and white
The craziest gummy that ever existed
But eating it could not be resisted
'That one looks bad,' said my mummy
'It will give you an awfully painful tummy.'

You see, the poor little gummy got a bad name
But really, inside, all gummies are the same
Just because his skin colour was rare
Doesn't mean his life should be unfair
So I went ahead and ate the gummy
And despite his colour, he tasted so yummy
So Mummy, your judgement was definitely out of place
Never judge a gummy bear until you've had a taste!

Clíodhna McDonald (14)
St Ronan's College, Lurgan

It's The Time Of Year

Spring! It's the time of year
Adorable lambs are born and light coats are worn
Days begin to get bright and Easter festivities are
full of delight

Summer! It's the time of year
The sweltering sun beats on the earth
And people begin to take to the waves to surf

Autumn! It's the time of year
Colourful leaves fall and we hear birds make their calls
A slight chill creeps into the air and Halloween jokers give us
a scare

Winter! It's the time of year
Christmas cheer is all around and snow is glistening
on the ground
Dark nights creep in fast; let's just hope they will last.

Sian Heaney (14)
St Ronan's College, Lurgan

Sports

Sport is great, it's good fun too,
There is definitely a sport that's right for you.
There are millions sports for you to do,
From basketball to rugby and hockey too.

It's great exercise and there's a lot to choose,
Like practising boxing when you're feeling the blues.
From dancing and prancing when you're feeling great
To learning new sports, like how to skate.

Running around a pitch and kicking a ball,
Shooting and scoring, the game's called football.

Basketball is definitely my favourite of all sports,
Running around with my mates, playing on the courts.

Mikey McCann (14)
St Ronan's College, Lurgan

Hope

Hopeful
But the glass is half empty
Hopeful
However, what degree do you need to foresee hope?
Hope does not come from the Pope
But from the heart
Pumping
Thumping
Deteriorating
Last breaths in the smoky air
But do you dare to stop?
Death does not define you
Hope defines you
Not everyone lives but the best
People have hope in their eyes
Twinkling
Sparkling
Retinas
Blinking
What do you see?
Hope or death?
The fine line is not within your mind
It is in the form of a blade
Don't slice away opportunity -
Have hope.

Aine Callaghan (16)
St Ronan's College, Lurgan

The Match Day

As I walk out on the pitch
Fans roaring my name
As I stand beside my best mate Mitch
We were all quite tame

As I walk out into the centre
As I shake the other captain's hand
As I remember the words of my mentor
The spectators watching from the stands

As I collect the ball
As I shoot
I switch the ball to Saul
The ball slides off my boot

The score ended up two-one
I was happy that we won
I switched tops with Paul
After the game I stuffed myself with buns.

Andrew Cooper (14)
St Ronan's College, Lurgan

Goodbye

Gunshots firing
Planes whistling as I run on
I see my best friend lying
A soldier beside him crying
All the memories rushing through my head
All the blood is pure red

Grenades booming
Soldiers screaming as I run on
I aim my gun down
As I am about to pull the trigger
My eyes are blinded by the sun
I see a running figure

Rats scampering
Rain pouring as I run on
I get into cover
Bullet fly by
I think of my lover
And I say goodbye.

Daire Kieran Campbell (14)
St Ronan's College, Lurgan

Forest Walk

Under the light of the rising sun
I wander aimlessly through the wood
Watching the foxes and hares as they run
Foraging for their food

I excitedly glimpse a trickling stream
I run up to it and leap across
As I land, I see a magpie gleam;
Standing atop a mound of moss

I suddenly realise that the sun is going down
It strikes me now that I must go
I glance around one last time with a frown
Can I come back? I do hope so.

Lauren Wilson
St Ronan's College, Lurgan

YOUNG WRITERS INFORMATION

We hope you have enjoyed reading this book – and that you will continue to in the coming years.

If you're a young adult who enjoys reading and creative writing, or the parent of an enthusiastic poet or story writer, do visit our website **www.youngwriters.co.uk.** Here you will find free competitions, workshops and games, as well as recommended reads, a poetry glossary and our blog.

If you would like to order further copies of this book, or any of our other titles, then please give us a call or visit **www.youngwriters.co.uk.**

Young Writers
Remus House
Coltsfoot Drive
Peterborough
PE2 9BF
(01733) 890066
info@youngwriters.co.uk